Patrick Droste/Ralf Strotmann

Telemark Skiing

Meyer & Meyer Sport

Original title: Telemark-Skifahren/Patrick Droste, Ralf Strotmann.
© Aachen: Meyer und Meyer, 2002
Translated by Peter Musch

British Library Cataloguing in Publication Data
A catalogue for this book is available from the British Library

Telemark Skiing / Patrick Droste, Ralf Strotmann.
– Oxford: Meyer und Meyer, (UK) Ltd., 2003
ISBN 1-84126-082-7

© 2003 by Meyer & Meyer Sport (UK) Ltd.
Aachen, Adelaide, Auckland, Budapest, Graz, Johannesburg,
Miami, Olten (CH), Oxford, Singapore, Toronto
 Member of the World
Sports Publishers' Association
www.w-s-p-a.org
Printed by Vimperk AG
ISBN 1-84126-082-7
E-Mail: verlag@m-m-sports.com
www.m-m-sports.com

CONTENTS

PREFACE

We, the two authors of this book, are far from being perfect Telemarkers. There sure are a huge number of freaks out there who are ripping the mountain way better than we, the two non-highlanders, do. But it is not at all important how good or bad someone stands on his teles – it is far more important to enjoy this unique feeling once you are cruising down the mountain down on your knees with your heel free. The only thing that counts is your broad grin. Nothing else.

As a consequence we want to bring this kind of winter sport to all those skiers who have not tried Telemark skiing before and give them a guideline to show them how simple and basic this turn actually is. We will introduce our readers to the material that is required for beginners and all those who want to convert to the ultimate way of gliding on two boards. Furthermore we want to give hints to good Telemarkers in order to improve and perfect their skiing – not as instructors, but out of our own experience. Also we are working on our performance with every turn we do. At least we want to remind the professionals about what they have already learned, or how they could have gotten there a lot easier.

This book should neither be a curriculum nor should it dictate how a specific motion, a turn or a technique has to be carried out. Everybody has the right – being a Telemarker: is obliged – to ski the way he or she gets the most fun. We are also far from claiming our approach to be the best way to teach and to learn Telemark skiing. We simply try to help those who are interested by giving them this little book and trying to show them how fast and easy everybody can learn the Telemark technique.

Since we know how much more fun it is to ski safely and under control, we have tried to collect a few good tips that might be helpful for Telemarkers of all skill levels.

Even though a hint that helps the one skier to improve his or her skiing by a hundred percent is of no use for the other – that's the reason why we attempted to find as many exercises and different approaches as possible, to satisfy everyone, from beginner to expert.

That's why it is very important not to lose patience and to ski as much as you can. This is the only way to get used to the enormous variety of movements, which are made possible through the free heel.

A lot of skiers never get to learn how important it is to work with their whole body in order to do a perfect turn. They ski with their head, instead of using their legs and knees and their torso. So don't think too much about what is right or wrong – just go out, get your skis and let it rock!

Throughout the whole book we will try to offer as many exercises as possible for each step. Nobody has to do boring repetitions to improve his skiing, but can gradually build up his skill level from beginner to expert in a pretty short time.

Normally it takes an intermediate to advanced alpine skier about one day to learn the basics of Telemarking. They might not be able to fly down double black runs after this, but they are freeheeling well enough to handle anything else that is groomed. You cannot take this for granted in every individual case, but our experience over the past years has shown us that at least nine out of ten students are having success along with these tips and the right instruction. That's something that we guarantee.

But before we get out into the snow, there are a few things that we have to have in mind: We will not (especially in the beginning of our Telemark career), be as fast as our friends on alpine equipment, we will fall more often, our legs will be sore and we will get addicted to Telemark skiing – just to have warned you.

You might not be a perfect Telemarker after having read this book. That is something we would never dare to claim. Maybe you just take the book along in your backpack on your next day skiing and have a little look any time you are sitting in a chair lift, or if you have a lunch break.

That's the way it is supposed to help you – read a little and then ski, ski, ski!

... and by the way, don't forget:
Have fun! Reading and even more importantly – Telemarking.

Patrick and Ralf

Around 1850 the Norwegians were the first to use the ski for fun

1 LOOK BACK

or a long time it was claimed that modern skiing was born in Morgedal in the Telemark region of Norway. Recent surveys have proved that other places in Norway are just as suited to bear this title. Therefore it is more correct to say that the whole of Norway has been the cradle of modern skiing.

Whether Sondre Ouversen NORHEIM was in fact the first one to ever do a Telemark turn cannot be answered either. But without any question, this farmer's son from Morgedal gave the most important impulses to the way we see modern skiing in our days – connected with fun, sport and competition.

It is in Norway where skis and skiing have been a part of living and working for many decades for the people who live there.

The high mountains, the deep fjords and the huge, snow covered plateaus have always been something to be managed by the Norwegians. As a consequence, skis were mainly used as a means of transportation and an important aid for hunting and fishing.

Also for Sondre NORHEIM, skis were something to make a living with as a farmer in Morgedal. In the course of time NORHEIM found his skis to be more than this – they became important for having fun with in his spare time.

Statue of Sondre NORHEIM at Morgedal, Norway

Sondre NORHEIM was born on the 10th of June 1825 in Morgedal and was raised on the Overbo farm, right above the little village. Even as a little child he had to give a hand to his parents on their farm. Together with his brother Eivind, he worked as a logger, shepherd and helped with the hay farming – but once his father gave him a pair of self-made skis when he was a little boy, all these kind of occupations started to bore him.

From this day on, Sondre started to neglect his duties and spent every minute he could on his boards instead – chasing through Morgedal, jumping off house roofs and cruising through the forests of his hometown. When Sondre turned 29, he got married to a young lady named Rannei. The people of Morgedal now expected him to become more quiet and reasonable and not to shred his skis like a madman anymore – but they were dead wrong. "Out there the mountains were calling and he had to answer" – like the Norwegian novelist Torjus LOUPEDALEN once wrote about Sondre NORHEIM.

Since the middle of the 19th century, something like a little ski scene established itself in Morgedal. On every Sunday the whole village was out to have fun in the snow. The younger people were flying across self-made kickers and wave sections and only got stopped by total darkness.

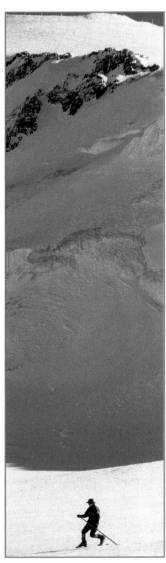

From 1870 on the Telemark style became the latest hype in the Norwegian mountain world

Torjus LOUPEDALEN described Morgedal in the year of 1850 like this: "The community houses roughly speaking 500 people, whom it has to feed and clothe, and provide work and leisure activities for. It cannot manage to feed them all; many must go out begging, and many others leave. (...) But the community can provide fun for them. There is dancing on the village green in the summer, skiing in the winter and the fiddle and dancing all year round. And here we have the key to it: the energy and go of the people in this community has to find release, expression, form — and they find it in skiing." (KLEPPEN 1986, 13)

It also was at this time when the term "Slalom" was created. Since alpine skiing had its first fans in the countries of the Alps, a lot of people tended to think that this word has its origin there — but this term has its roots in the dialect of the Telemark region. The first syllable "Sla" stands for slope, whereas the "track" through the snow is indicated with "lam". An even more daring variant of this "Sla-lam" leads in a wild run through ditches and gorges, full of bushes and rocks and through the trees, with a hair's breadth. Such "dangerous" tracks were the ultimate challenge for the people of Morgedal — similar to the excitement of the free ride and world cup races of our days.

It all started with jumps over self-made kickers in the 19th century

But let us get back to our friend Sondre. In the year of 1866 he participated in his first competition. In the neighbor village of Ofte, in Hoydalsmo, the first ski jump competition of Norway was held — and the winner was Sondre NORHEIM, who is told to have yelled "first prize" right after his landing.

It took him another two years to get really famous — this was when he won the Iversloken championships at the Aker-church in Christiania, the former

Oslo. This race was a combination of jumping, cross country, downhill and slalom. What counted most was the fastest overall time. Nevertheless there were a few judges at particular places who rated style and performance as well. This race in the year of 1868 had a starting field of 50 competitors from all over Norway. Sondre was at this time 43 years old and had one most of the way between Morgedal and the capital on his skis, before he went up the hill to the start.

He always finished his jumps in the Telemark position – everybody in his hometown did so and in Morgedal this seemed to be the most natural way to land – only in Christiania this way to land was something that really amazed the spectators. Until then, a jump was performed with bent knees and landed with the skis in parallel position.

From then on, the Telemark landing became the ideal way of finishing a jump. Sondre used to jump in a perfect upright position and only did a step once he landed. Same as his skiing. In the step position he let the inner ski come to a half-plow – which gave him much more control than the so far used *Christiania turn* – in which the skis were torn sideways. This turning in a step position is known as the *Telemark turn* today.

This is what a journalist wrote in the "Aftenbladet" right after the competition: "It was the winner of the 1st prize who excelled over all the other competitors. He has such a remarkable style of skiing that one would think he had to be born to it, and that it was his natural way of moving around. With the ski pole like a walking stick in one hand, and his cap in the other, he started off down the hill at top speed – then suddenly he jumped, so that his skis did not touch the ground for 2 or 3 ski lengths.

When he landed after such a jump there was not a trace of unsteadiness or lack of balance. Only when one has seen Sondre Ouversen Norheim and recalls that the man is now 43 years old, can one begin to imagine what such a first-class skier would be able to accomplish in his prime time." (from KLEPPEN 1986, 28)

On the 8th of March in the same year, Sondre did a jump of 30 meters – a width that had not been thought possible at this time.

The people who lived in the Telemark region heard the call of the mountains year round

From 1870 on, the Telemark style was absolutely "in". Everybody wanted to learn this elegant and smooth style – gliding down the runs with a free heel and bent knees. Sondre, who stopped competing at the age of fifty, founded the first ski school in 1881 in Norway's capital, to teach the city folks everything he knew about skiing. By doing this, he released a real "avalanche". Next to tobogganing and ice-skating, skiing became Norway's #1 sport. Organized races and competitions were held and skiing became the first winter discipline of the Olympic games.

"Telemark is the rightful home of skiing. The people of Telemark are unquestionably our country's best skiers, and if they are the best in our country, I can doubtlessly say, without fear of exaggeration, that they are also the world's best. They have taught the townspeople a completely new way of skiing, and have thereby raised the art of skiing to the heights it has achieved in recent years. Telemark skiers truly deserve our respect and thanks." (Fridtjof NANSEN (1861-1930), 1886, in: KLEPPEN 1986, 8)

Sondre NORHEIM was not only an excellent skier, but also had a lot of skills as a craftsman. In his early years he had already developed a ski which later on became known as the Telemark ski. This ski, which he built out of spruce wood, already had something that is nowadays known as side-cut – having a wider tip, a narrower center and again a wider tail. As he found out, it was a lot easier to do turns with this ski, which had a side-cut of 15 mm (84-69-79), than on conventionally shaped boards. Besides, his ski, with the length of 2.4 m, had been a lot shorter than the boards used so far (3 m).

In the course of time, these skis were gradually changed. For cross-country use they had a narrower shape, whereas for jumping they tended to be even wider. The only thing that remained unchanged was the side-cut. All skis that had a waist were called Telemark skis until the 1940s. As skis with a "built in curve" were rediscovered around 1990, they were called Carving skis.

But Sondre did not only invent the world's first carving ski – he also made some incredible inventions concerning bindings about a hundred and fifty years ago. Until 1850 it was common to fix the ski to the boot only with a toe piece – but what does fix mean? The forefoot was slid into a toe strap, but this solution could not offer much in the way of better ski control.

Sondre started thinking and experimenting and came to develop the world's first binding with a heel fixation, which simply was a cord going around the heel part of the boot. Around Morgedal, people at first thought that Sondre had gone completely nuts.

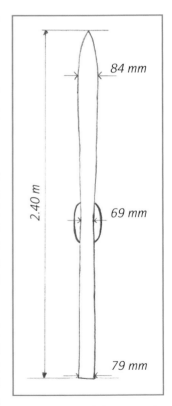

A Telemark ski from Sondre NORHEIMS time, with a side-cut of 15 mm (84-69-79)

Nobody could imagine that there was a need to fix your feet this tight to the skis. But with the binding, it became possible to jump without losing ones skis in the air and to do controlled turns – and this finally was the precondition for the modern ski sport.

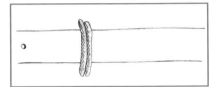 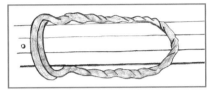

A binding from the first half of the 19th century (left) and a model of Sondre NORHEIM's with a heel fixation from 1850 (right)

At the end of the 19th century, a lot of inhabitants from the Telemark region – as well as Sondre NORHEIM and his wife Rannei – emigrated to the USA or Canada and brought skiing to the new world.

In the course of time the landing technique developed into a turning technique

Sondre NORHEIM ended up in North Dakota, where he died in 1897, at the age of 72 years. Rannei survived her husband for 32 years and died in 1929 at the age of 104. Before his death, Sondre NORHEIM and all the other Norwegians must have brought out a good seed, since Telemarking had its renaissance in the 1970s right in the US.

It was in 1971 when five mountain guides from Crested Butte, Colorado rediscovered the Telemark technique while researching the history of skiing. It was more of a coincidence that Doug BUZELL, Craig HALL, Greg DAILBY, Jack MARCIAL and Rick BORCOVEC at this time found the book of Stein ERIKSEN "Come Ski With Me". Here, they learned everything about Stein's father, Marius, from the Telemark region of Norway and the Telemark turn and were inspired to try this old technique by themselves.

BORCOVEC, at this time director of the Nordic Adventure Ski School in Crested Butte, remembered their first attempts to get away from the lift served terrain, into the ungroomed deep snow and the backcountry. As a consequence, they started to experiment with their randonee ski gear and open bindings, to find out pretty soon that the usual alpine technique is not at all suited as long as they were skiing with a free heel. "It was five American ski instructors and mountain skiers who started digging into the history of Norwegian skiing and unearthed the Morgedal technique. Doug BUZZELL, Craig HALL, Greg DALBEY, Jack MARCIAL and Rick BORCOVEC were at that time in Crested Butte, Colorado, and had read the book "Come Ski With Me" by Stein ERIKSEN.

There they read about his father Marius and the Telemark turn, and this inspired them to try it out in open country. BORCOVEC, the director of the Nordic Adventure Ski School, has said about these first experiments that it was the need to get away from the ski lifts and out into open, virgin skiing country that made them start to experiment. In 1971 they tried touring skis with loose bindings, and soon found out that ordinary alpine techniques were unsuitable in deep powder snow and mixed terrain. "The snowplow was difficult in deep powder snow, and the parallel turn too unstable on free-heeled bindings with flexible boots. So we based the Telemark style on a photograph seen of Stein Eriksen's father demonstrating the Telemark turn. With this photograph as the starting point we went on our own." (BORCOVEC, in: KLEPPEN 1986, 12). With reference to Rick BORCOVEC'S memories, the American ski historic Art BURROWS writes, "Little did these five know that taking up this skiing technique again would lead to a renaissance of Telemark skiing. Its growing popularity marks the end of an era of specialization, and for many people the Telemark style is the best kind of skiing." (KLEPPEN 1986, 12)

The wave of popularity was rolling back to Norway in the seventies, where many skiers rediscovered the enormous versatility of "their" old, new winter sport. Nowadays Telemark skiing, not only in Scandinavia but as well in the European Alps, has developed into an popular alternative to alpine skiing and snowboarding, gaining more and more fans.

The number of ski fans rediscovering this old technique is constantly growing. Nostalgic persons, traditionalists, freaks, racers and outdoor people meet here – and get along great.

Nowadays more and more skiers get enthusiastic about the old Norwegian technique

The right equipment is the key to fun and success for Telemarking

2 EQUIPMENT

Since its renaissance in the seventies, the old Norwegian technique really has a hard time developing itself in the Alps. Only very few skiers could handle the skinny boards, the soft leather boots and the bindings, which were miles away from the safety standards of alpine gear, and hardly distinguished from the equipment that Sondre NORHEIM was using.

This situation has changed dramatically in our days and the new material gives almost every skier the chance to enjoy the fascination of Telemarking. Modern Telemark boots are made out of plastic, are as stable as alpine boots and come with all their fancy details: canting, forward lean, walking mechanisms, power straps and so on. There hardly is a difference between Telemark and alpine skis anymore and even alpine skis are used for Telemarking pretty often; but also there have been quite a few changes in the last few years for Telemark bindings.

Now there is a new generation of releasable bindings on the market that have seriously improved the safety standard of Telemark skiing. They give the beginner and intermediate more confidence in the new equipment and allow the advanced and expert skier to ski faster and more stylishly.

Even though it became more and more difficult to differentiate Telemarking from alpine skiing by the equipment, there still is one thing which at least stands for the kick of our sport: the free heel. This tiny, yet huge difference is what makes the tele-gear so unique and special.

With the perfect material there are no limits for the Telemarker

2.1 Boots

There are not too many things anymore that distinguish a Telemark from an alpine boot except the flex fold in the toe part and the prolonged shoe tip for the 75 mm norm-binding.

Until 1990 tele-boots were made exclusively out of leather. This material was flexible enough to be bent in the toe part of the foot, but contrary to the alpine models, the leather boots would not give sufficient stability and performance to the skier – they were too soft and tended to wear out way too fast. Adding torsional rigidity by supplying the boots with plastic reinforcements and additional buckles was tried, which worked pretty well. But nevertheless – these leather boots would not give enough hold and transmit the power onto the ski properly. This is the reason why leather was replaced by plastic as boot building material in the nineties of the last century.

Different types of Telemark boots (from right to left): a leather boot for backcountry touring, a soft plastic randonée boot and a stiff plastic boot for on- and off-piste skiing.

But still leather is not "out". There are a lot of traditionalists out there who still believe that the old Norwegian technique requires an old fashioned boot – but not only these "fundamentalists" trust in leather. It is still first choice for backcountry touring and cross-country hikes for which the ideal boot has to be soft, low, light-weight and comfortable.

Those Telemarkers who prefer higher speeds and more radical lines only have one choice: plastic. These plastic boots offer more edge control and a firmer hold, together with a more direct transmission of power. Telemark skiers can now ski on the limit in any terrain: moguls, deep snow, as well as steep and icy groomed slopes – same speed, same line as alpine skiers, different weapon. But not only advanced and expert skiers profit from the advantages that this new generation of boots has to offer. Especially beginners now have the chance to learn the basics of the Telemark turn, five times faster than before. Wearing plastic boots does not only enable them to "Feel the terrain", according to a slogan of the Italian boot manufacturer Crispi, but helps them to get used to the new free heel situation a lot faster than before and still allows them to "feel the ski".

The first plastic boot was produced in 1990-91 by the Italian company Scarpa and was at this time hardly accepted by the majority of the tele-skiers. Nowadays a plastic boot is simply part of modern equipment, whereas the different models and brands have gone through serious research and developmental work in the past ten years. The materials used became stiffer and little things like canting control, forward lean adjustment, or micro tuning buckles and thinsulate liners were added to improve the overall performance.

The specialization in Telemarking mirrors itself also in boot technology. As a consequence, companies like Crispi, Garmont or Scarpa offer boots for any particular use. Race boots, which have a high, hard and tight cut guarantee maximum control in terms of edging and turning. Touring boots, which are softer, lighter and lower, offer more wearing comfort and are mainly intended to be used as a compromise between a pure backcountry hiking model and an on-piste performance shell. All-round boots, which are a mixture between a race and a touring boot, according to their height and stiffness, cover the spectrum from on-piste to deep snow and are good for skiers of all levels. The different boot brands on the market differentiate themselves generally speaking in the variety of fits they have to offer. Scarpa boots are good for narrow to normally shaped feet with a lower arch, whereas Crispi's and Garmont's are good for wider feet with higher arches.

But there are also boots specifically designed for the shape of female feet as a contribution to the growing number of free heeling women. Last but not least, there are kid's models on the market, allowing even the youngsters to have the most fun possible in the snow.

Nowadays there also is equipment on the market that is specifically designed for Telemarking women

2.2 Skis

Before the stiff plastic boots and the wide carving skis were on the market, the difference between Telemark and alpine skis was enormous.

A Telemark ski was pretty similar to a normal cross-country ski until the nineties: Extremely narrow, with a waist of about 54 mm and a tip of about 72 mm – but at least they had edges and could be skied, with some experience, on hard packed and groomed slopes, too.

Skiing on regular alpine skis has at this time been a real challenge, but actually was the only alternative to keep up with your alpine skiing buddies, for at least half a day.

Have you ever tried to skate on your longboard with flip-flops? This comes pretty close to skiing a 1.95 m slalom ski with soft leather boots.

In the meantime, all this belongs in the past. Depending on the intended use, nowadays you can use almost every alpine ski for Telemarking.

Only for backcountry skiing and longer tours in the wilderness is it useful to go back to the skinny boards – due to their lightweight construction, they simply have better performance when it comes to walking and covering great distances in ungroomed terrain.

Different types of Telemark skis (from left to right): Narrow backcountry ski, wide and soft free ride ski and an all-round ski with a moderate side-cut.

But if your main aim is to ski on groomed slopes or go freeriding, you only have one choice again: modern carving skis with a side-cut. They offer, similar to the plastic boots, far more control, flotation and turn performance. Opposite to alpine carvers, Telemark carving skis have a softer tip and a little less weight. This is due to the fact that for a free heel skier it is quite a bit more difficult to get pressure on the front part of the ski.

Same as for alpine skis, there are models with different side-cuts and uses in the Telemark section. Why carving skis with a side-cut? As Sondre NORHEIM had already found out 140 years ago, it is a lot easier to initiate and to steer a turn along the side-cut of these boards – plus it's more precise, more controlled and takes less effort, no matter how fast you are skiing.

Anyway, skis are lot shorter nowadays than they were back in the 70s and 80s – at this time Telemark skis had to have a length between 1.95 and 2.10 m. Today, skis hardly ever exceed the length of 1.90 m – a regular all-round carver has between 1.65 and 1.85 m, race skis vary around 1.80 and 1.90 m and free ride skis differ between 1.75 and 1.85 m.

For skiing on groomed slopes, it is preferable to use skis with a moderate to extreme side-cut, like Black Diamond's *Arc Demon* (99/66/ 92 mm), the K2 *Super Stinx* (107/70/97), or the K2 *Worldpiste* 14/78/105).

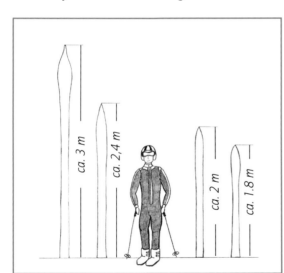

Different ski lengths: 3 m (9 feet!) around 1800, 2.40 m at the time of NORHEIM, 2 m between 1980 and 1990 and 1.80 m today.

Skiing in the fall line in Telemark position

For novices, but also for Telemarkers who primarily ski on lift served terrain, any all-round carver does a perfect job, due to the easy turn initiation and the good tracking.

More and more Telemarkers now have their playgrounds in the ungroomed and the deep snow and therefore prefer fat and super fat skis with side-cuts like the Black Diamond *Arc Angel* (107/71/99), the *Mira* (110/78/100) or the K2 *Work Stinx* (118/88/105). These skis have a really wide tip, offering maximum flotation and performance in the deep and steep, but still enough side-cut to be skiable on hardpacked and groomed snow.

For the new school shredders among the Telemarkers there are now twin-tip boards on the market, which are not only performing extremely well in the half pipe, but also are really versatile and quick turning skis for on- and off-piste. Check out the example, the K2 *Piste Pipe* (107/75/98).

Last but not least, there are also the so called "Telemark race skis" on the market, which come with a stiffer tip and tail, have a pretty strong side-cut and are narrower than the other models. Most of the racers prefer to ski on alpine slalom or short slalom carvers, since they simply outperform any of the Telemark models in their race suitability.

To summarize, one can say that in future it will get more and more difficult to differentiate between alpine and Telemark skis. The main difference simply will be the intended use: race, carving, off-piste and freeride touring.

Basically we don't care whether we are standing on Telemark skis, or on alpine skis which only have a better selling Telemark design – as long as they are versatile, easy to release, super stable in the hardpacked crud, can stick hard landings and help us to rip all "da fixed heelers 'round".

2.3 Bindings

Until the year 2000 there haven't been too many changes and improvements ithe Telemark binding sector. The binding types which were used since the Telemark revival in the seventies, weren't particularly different from what Sondre NORHEIM had, far over a hundred years ago. Fortunately there have been quite a few improvements in the last two years.

But first we want to talk about the "classics", such as the 3-Pin and a few cable bindings. The biggest advantage of a 3-Pin binding is the incomparable freedom of movement. There is no spring, no cable and no heel lever which gets into your way. Mainly for ski touring and in the deep snow, you learn to appreciate the advantages of such a simple piece of equipment.

You don't feel any resistance during the climb and thus save a lot of power and effort – skiing in deep snow, you have a very centered position, because there is no cable which pulls you back and by this gives you unintended   pressure on your tips. The disadvantages of the 3-Pin are: For doing high speed turns on a groomed slope, you lack side stability and tracking – and the worst thing that can happen is:

If you have a hard fall, your pin holes simply get torn out and you sure have a hard time to fix them skis back on your boots again. But here comes a little tip for all the *pinheads* out there: Go to a hardware store, buy six metal cartridges and fix them right into the little holes. Problem solved.

Different Telemark bindings:
3-Pin binding for ski touring
and deep snow (left),
cable binding for groomed slopes

Another choice of bindings that you can rely on are those with the cables such as the *G3*, the *Voile Hardwire*, the *Rainey Superloop* and *Hammerhead* and the *Rottefella Cobra* (the *Voile* and the *Rottefella* don't come with a cable but with a steel rod, but have the same functioning principle).

The advantage of these systems is the very good stability they provide for the heel. Similar to a 3-Pin, the boot is fixed in a toe piece and an additional cable or steel rod holds your heel. This means that you definitely feel a pull from your boot towards your ski, which really helps beginners and novices because they don't have to ski as precisely as with a 3-Pin.

Modern release bindings let you survive even a crash like this

But good Telemarkers who ski a lot on groomed slopes and in freeski terrain also appreciate the advantages and the stability of cable bindings.

Next to the improved stability, these bindings provide the advanced and expert Telemarker with more pressure, which goes right into the exact and controlled steering of the skis. A little disadvantage can be that it always takes a bit of fumbling to get into these cable bindings once your fingers are cold and wet – but why Telemark, if you need a step-in?

The improvements we were talking about in the Telemark binding sector mainly focus on a new product on the market since the 2000-2001 season, the German *7tm*. This innovative system offers not only an awesome skiing performance but also is the only product on the market that is a CE-certified safety binding, which releases sideways and in case of a frontal impact.

2.4 Poles

In the early years of Telemark skiing people were using a long, single pole (known as a lurk), which gave support and helped them to keep balance. But pretty soon, this single pole was replaced by two poles out of bamboo cane, with baskets and two leather straps. Today carbon is used instead of bamboo, the baskets are made out of plastic and the straps out of nylon. Since there are no particular Telemarking poles on the market, you can use any alpine pole, which should have a basket that is big enough to support your pole plant in the deep snow. If you plan to ski tour, it makes sense to buy adjustable ones – our personal recommendation: get any of the Black Diamond poles which have a so called "Flick lock" mechanism for the length adjusting, because it really holds. Opinions about the best length for Telemark poles differ widely – the best thing is to try yourself, but in general your poles don't have to be longer or shorter as for alpine skiing.

Away from the crowds and up there in the mountains you need reliable equipment

2.5 Accessories

Besides boots, skis, bindings and poles there are quite a few other things you definitely need, or which are at least pretty useful. First essential accessory, as long as you don't use ski brakes, is a ski leash.

Never risk that your skis run away after a fall that pulled your boots out of the bindings – in a lot of ski areas the use of leashes is obligatory, because run away skis already have caused terrible accidents!

Also in the deep snow, it is of great advantage to have your skis connected to your boots after a fall where they came off.

Many Telemarkers don't even put their skis on without having protected their knees with suitable pads – just bang your patella into a rock or onto one of your skis once and you know why!

Use inline skating or moto cross kneepads and wear them underneath your ski pants, they are just for insurance: Once you have 'em, you mostly don't need 'em.

Same thing goes for the helmet. It not only protects you if you drop over a 15 m cliff, or if you free-ski in Alaska – it also gives you a solid protection on icy slopes and in races, plus it really looks sweet.

3 TELE TECHNIQUE

Please buckle up, now it's getting serious. We start learning one of the most beautiful winter sports in the world. At this, we are trying to convey this old, new technique without damaging nor overloading the movement apparatus – first of all we want to have big time fun. We are making use of the modern equipment, the terrain and our natural movement possibilities to learn as fast and effortlessly as possible.

An experienced Telemarker is of great help for every novice learning the new technique

Our experiences of the last few years have proved that mainly experienced alpine skiers, looking for a new challenge, are attracted to Telemark skiing. Therefore we can assume that we don't have to deal with absolute beginners – we rather teach folks with experiences about gliding, edging, turns and so on and therefore will concentrate mainly on the conveying of Telemark specific elements.

We don't want to cram you full with complicated movement analysis, but rather reduce the learning of Telemark technology to the essentials. This means that in beginner training we are leaving out the movement example "high – low", because the step change or transition automatically has a vertical component which is done anyway and does not have to be explained.

The next thing that our pupils or readers have to get used to is the fact that they will not be confronted with terms like *"right"* or *"wrong"*. What is right, what is wrong? A technique that takes a Telemarker down the hill, never can be wrong – therefore we are using terms like: more *effective, effortless, safer, more controlled, faster, or easier.*

We have divided the exercise program into two main parts. First, novices can learn skills like the Telemark position and first forms of Telemark turning, in a basic training with four steps. At the same time, those who transfer from alpine skiing should – and can – be led to their aim on a direct way.

Based on the already achieved knowledge of alpine skiing, more and more Telemark specific skills are going to be introduced in the series of exercises. The learning steps are arranged so that even Telemark novices are able to do easy to intermediate runs after a few exercises of the Telemark technique. Skiing experience has a matter of priority in these four steps:

There is to be little standing and talking on the slope, but instead a lot of skiing and practicing. Once these basics exist, the wide world of Telemarking is open to the new freeheeler. He can now find out the innumerable possibilities of Telemark skiing by carving, short turning, mogul and deep snow skiing and ski touring.

Both the basic- and the pro-training (action and fun), are respectively built up after the same scheme – first you get a description of what you are already supposed to know (prerequisites, or what I can do), then we list up the skills that we are aiming for (learning targets, or what I want to learn) and finally, what you have to do to get there and a few intensifying exercises for every learning step.

3.1 Basics

3.1.1 Step 1:

Getting Used to the Free Heel and the Telemark Position on Even Ground

In this learning phase the novice should get used to the new equipment, learn the Telemark position while standing and through this find a stable position of the body.

I. Getting used to the new equipment

What I can do
- The Telemark novice has experiences in alpine skiing. He can keep the balance, glide, drift, turn and edge.

What I want to learn
- First of all the Telemarker-to-be has to get used to the new material. Therefore, he has to get used to the primarily unfamiliar binding. Beware that there is, according to the asymmetrical shape of boots and bindings, a left and a right side, which is indicated through the mounting of the ski leashes on the outside of the ski, or with little arrows on the toe pieces of 3-pin bindings.

How I can learn it
- Lean backward and forward in a standing position.
- Get down on your knees and try to grab the ski tips with your hands.
- Try to stand on both tips of your boots at the same time.
- Slide your ski back and forth and try to get a feeling for the free heel.
- Jump up.
- Try to run like a cross-country skier.
- Climb up in a herring bone or in a side step.
- Step around the tips or the ends of your skis.
- Chasing games.

- Ski down a moderate slope in alpine technique.
- Ski alpine while standing on your toe tips only.

Standing on the tips of your boots

Grabbing your ski tips with your hands

II. How to learn the Telemark position

A proper position is the core of Telemark skiing, whereas the step position and the upper body are of the same importance. Different to alpine skiing, the ski position is unparalleled – one ski is pushed forward , the other one is pushed back. The distance between both feet is about one sole length – this distance can vary individually and is only used as a guideline. So is the vertical orientation of the upper body. One skier prefers a higher, the other one, a lower position – in the end it all is Telemark and you can ski awesome turns in both positions.

The position of the upper body depends on the personal preference of the skier, but is also influenced by snow conditions, steepness of the slope and the turn radii. A good Telemarker should always be able to adapt to the situation and master all positions.

The perfect Telemark position

The lowering of the body's center of gravity guarantees a stable and compact position, which nevertheless is pretty exhausting. Once the center of gravity is higher, you can initiate turns faster and easier, the knees' weight load is minimized (better bending angle) and you have more room to absorb strokes and bumps. The knee of the forward ski should never be totally straight , since the overall position is getting too stiff and the shock absorbing function disappears.

It is just as important to keep the upper body quiet. Every superfluous movement immediately transfers itself to the skis. You usually notice this as soon as your skis start to slide away underneath your body and as a consequence you crash. Therefore you should always have an eye on a reasonable and last but not least effective upper body position. If this is given, your whole body is in balance, your skis can be controlled optimally and power can be transferred effectively.

The whole posture should be loose and ready to move. Imagine you are a soccer goalkeeper waiting for a penalty kick: You stand on both feet and are ready for action, for a jump, or in our case, for a turn. Therefore you should never freeze in a position. That's what we are looking for. Telemarking is a dynamic movement along with loading and unloading, tilting, turning and a vertical movement. At the beginning of a Telemark career it is indicated to do most or all exercises without poles. Through this, the novice has to take an optimal position without the support of his poles.

What I have to do

- Front leg (downhill ski) with a strongly bent knee and hip, almost no bending in the ankle joint.
- Front foot weighted on the whole sole of the foot.
- Back foot with the heel up, standing not on your toe tips but on the whole forefoot.
- Back foot right underneath your butt.
- Back leg (uphill ski) with strongly bent knee and ankle joint, almost no bending in the hip.
- Back knee is as high as the center of the lower leg of the front leg.

- Distance between the front and the back leg is about a sole length.
- Parallel open ski position/wide stance: distance between the skis is, depending on the situation, as wide as your hip or as wide as your hand. If the position is too tight, the advantages of the open ski position (e.g. edging) are of no value.
- Upper body is upright or slightly bent forward.

How I can learn it
- Welcome game: group is running about, meeting another novice means jumping into a step position, clapping his shoulder, call his name.
- Fencing game: Two Telemarkers are facing each other in a step position and are fencing with their poles (hold your poles upside down, danger of injury!).

Fencing game

- Sit on the thighs of the Telemarker behind you.
- Balance games: Who is able to stand longest in a step position on his back or on his front leg (crane position)?
- Chasing games: Who gets caught "petrifies" in a step position and is set free again with a clap from another skier.
- Finding of the Telemark position while standing according to the above mentioned movement without skis.
- Finding of the Telemark position while standing according to the above mentioned movement with skis.
- Shifting from one into the other Telemark position with/without poles.
- Jumping from one into the other Telemark position with/without poles.

- Contrast exercise while standing: big step and little step, high and low step position, upper body bent forward and backward.

Contrast exercise: big and little step

Contrast exercise: high and low position

Even with the novices you can watch the most different Telemark positions. One prefers a deeper step position, whereas the other appreciates a little higher stand. There sure is an ideal position, which is pretty helpful as a guideline. But anyway, nobody should be forced into a certain movement. Every Telemarker has different physical prerequisites or prefers his individual style for esthetic reasons. In Telemarking, this is not only permitted, but particularly desired.

3.1.2 Step 2:
Improve the Telemark Position when Skiing

All these standing exercises cannot make a real Telemarker happy any longer. He wants to ski – and that's exactly what we do now. First a little remark: Crashes and falls are part of the game and no beginner should let occasional snow contact drive him crazy or even discourage him:

There is no such thing like Telemarking without crashes (ever heard of tele-crashin' or tele-wreckin'?) and plus that, the falls hardly ever ache. According to the free heel you hardly have any resistance or a lever to your ankle, knee and hip joints and as a consequence the risk of an injury is minimized and the residual risk is almost eliminated by release bindings of the latest generation.

But let's stop talking about crashes. After having done all these exercises in the stand, we sure will do well on the piste – skiing! First thing we want to try is gliding in the fall line - which is the same line a ball takes once it is rolling down a hill – the shortest and most direct way from top to bottom.

Crashes and falls are simply a part of Telemarking – for beginners as well as for experts

A good position on the ski is the key to success for good and safe Telemarking

After first experiences in the fall line, we are moving to a wide and groomed slope with a mellow grade to practice the Telemark position in the traverse. This appears to be more difficult in the beginning, since now the gravity output of the slope does not have an even but a one-sided effect on the body. Make sure that not only the position of your upper body is well balanced and that the Telemark step is wide enough, but that you have as well at least 30% of your weight on your back ski.

A Telemark novice with alpine skiing experience is used to put weight on the downhill ski and thus, on the whole foot, from heel to toe. Therefore the load of the front boot/ski rarely is a problem – mostly it is difficult for a novice to put enough weight on the back or on the inside ski. We will pay special attention to this in the following learning sequence. In any case it is important that the back foot is right underneath your butt, no matter whether you have a higher or lower position, or whether you ski with a shorter or a longer step. It is also of great importance that your back foot has weight on the whole forefoot and not only on the toe tips – this is the only way to transfer the pressure optimally to the ski. The back ski is not only dragged behind the front ski, but it should be weighted as active and as effective as the front ski.

Similar as in modern alpine skiing, you should aim to have an open ski position, or a wide stance, meaning that the side distance between both skis should be at least a hand's width. Depending on the steepness of the slope and the snow conditions, this varies up to hip-wide, but 10-20 cm can be regarded as a good all-round width for the beginner. With a narrower ski position the whole body position gets pretty unstable, you have to check your balance again and again and an effective edging of the skis is almost impossible – but don't let the distance get too wide, because then you have to ski on two different levels.

What I can do
- Having control of the Telemark position in the stand.

What I want to learn
- Having control of the Telemark position going straight down or traversing.
- Open ski position with best weight distribution possible on both skis.

What I have to do
- Learn and improve the Telemark position in motion.
- Wide stance.
- Weight skis equally.
- Upper body facing into the direction of travel.
- Arms slightly bent, hands on belly height in front of the upper body.

How I can learn it
- Go straight down a slope with a slight incline and a long out-run (maybe even with a back stretch) in alpine position and try to glide in the Telemark position for a few meters.
- Try to make the gliding sequences in the Telemark position longer and longer and practice on both sides.
- Competition: Who can glide through a gate built from ski poles in a deep Telemark position? Who glides furthest in the Telemark position? Who can jump a little kicker and land in the Telemark position?
- Gliding contrast exercise: low/high position, short/long step, leaning backward/forward with your upper body.
- Jump into the Telemark position while traversing a slope alpine style.

- Try to glide into the Telemark position while traversing a slope; stop at the end of the traverse, turn and start again.
- Try to find the optimal position for traversing through contrast exercises – low/high, short/long.
- Partner exercise: You have three positions (1: very upright, 2: neutrally upright, 3: very low) and once the one behind shouts the numbers, you are trying to get into the proper position.
- Another contrast exercise can be: upper body twists downhill, uphill and frontal into the direction of travel; lower your chin onto your chest or raise it while skiing; ski on your uphill/downhill ski only, ski on both skis.
- Competition: Who can sit on his heel while traversing? Who can push his back knee down on the ski?

Sitting on the heel

Touching the ski with the back knee

- Remain in Telemark position while sliding down sideways in steep terrain.
- Practice the Telemark position without poles while traversing.

Skiing without poles

- Skiing without poles: Draw a line through the snow with your uphill hand on the uphill side, draw a line with your uphill hand on the downhill side, draw a line with your downhill hand on the uphill side, draw a line with both hands on both sides.
- Motivation ride: Practice the Telemark position in traverses and connect them with alpine turns.

Drawing a line in the snow with your hand

Even after a lot of Telemark exercises, mostly less experienced skiers still feel pretty wobbly with the free heel. This uncertainty usually expresses itself by the fact that they execute only a very small step. They unconsciously go back to their well-known and approved movement model of alpine skiing, in which both feet are kept together tightly all the time. But for Telemarking this definitely is the wrong approach into the wrong direction, because the smaller the step position is carried out, the smaller the standing surface becomes and the instability gets all the worse.

Typical beginner fault: Step position too small

Another typical fault is the stripping, or over-rotating, towards the slope while skiing across the fall line. The reason is that the pelvis axis is lined up towards the mountain through the step position and that alpine skiers automatically take their shoulder into the turn with a sweep. As a correction measure, these novices should counter-rotate their shoulders intentionally and line up their upper body towards the valley.

Typical beginner fault: Twisted upper body

Awesome learning aid: Slalom pole

In order to help also the "problem child", to overcome his initial uncertainties and to make him a good Telemarker in the end, you just give him a hand, with the help of a slalom pole. With a good and experienced tele-skier or a ski instructor at the other end, he can practice the positions (step position, upper body) at due leisure. This way of practicing is of a greater value than being confronted with a load of technical terms and instructions.

3.1.3 Step 3:

Getting Used to Directional Changes in the Telemark Position

If slopes would be endlessly wide we could traverse along the fall line for hours – but on the one hand this is endlessly boring and on the other hand, due to the one-sided load, pretty exhausting. As a consequence it is only natural to descend a slope by doing turns – and that's our topic in step 3 of the basic training.

Just like flying: Telemark turns

The step change or transition serves as a basis for directional changes in Telemark and has to be learned first. This step into a new direction means nothing else actually than each of us knows from daily walking: One foot swings in front, the other one swings back. Therefore we will pick up this well-known movement and do the transition for the Telemark turn by pushing the rear foot forcefully forward. Once this action is mastered, we will try to put more dynamics into this movement, by pushing the back foot forward and the front foot back with a sweep. Through this, the typical Telemark transition, which is a fluent movement, would be performed. In a second learning unit we will put the main emphasis on directional changes. Based on the transition we will practice doing turns. Using the pole plant as a prelude movement prior to the transition and the following turn, step 3 is finished.

What I can do
- Skiing in the Telemark position across and in the fall line.

What I want to learn
- Transition.
- Directional change from the fall line.
- Turn over the fall line.
- Pole plant.

What I have to do
- At the transition, the front ski is pushed back and the back ski pushed forward simultaneously. This movement should be carried out as fluently and dynamically as possible. The transition can be connected with a slight straightening up of the whole body.
- To do a turn, the outer leg is getting pushed forward, the inner leg is getting pushed backward. The turn is initiated with a slight tilting of the upper body into the center of the turn, or a slight prerotation of the upper body into the new direction and a forward-inward movement of the legs. The turn is carried out across the fall line into a traverse through a measured out use of the edges (drifts).

How I can learn it
- Practice the transition standing, without skis. Jump from one Telemark position into the other, while doing the transition in the air.
- Practice the transition standing, with skis. Only pull the back leg forward, only pull the front leg back; pull both legs back and forth at the same time; do the transition with a jump (both skis are in the air).
- Practice the transition while going straight down the hill; try the same while going switch (backwards).
  Shoving: Straighten up, as if you are walking; try small and great steps; find your own rhythm.
  Jumping: Change without interruption.
- Practice the transition in the traverse.
  Shoving: Try to move up from the Telemark position to the alpine position, take a break and go down again; try to carry out this change more and more fast and fluently.

Jumping across a pole to learn the transition

Jumping: Jump across a pole in the snow with a step turn.

- Uphill christie in Telemark position: Traverse a little more diagonal, start going downhill, turn uphill and come through tilting, prerotation and a forward-inward movement of your knees to a stand.
- Ski down in the fall line in Telemark position, then do a turn until you are facing uphill again – now try the other side (if the left leg is in front you do a turn to the right and vice versa)
- Ski down in the fall line in alpine position, go down into a Telemark position and do a turn right in this moment (almost the same exercise as before, only a little more dynamically).

Start in an alpine position in the fall line, go down into a Telemark position and change directions

- Motivation ride: Traverse in Telemark position, initiate the turn in alpine position, finish the turn in Telemark position, next turn.

Traverse in Telemark position, alpine turn initiation, finish the turn in Telemark position

Now we put the single kits "transition" and "directional change" together:

- Big step with the so far uphill ski (or outside ski) into the new direction.
- Practice the transition in a traverse for four times, initiate the turn with the fifth and do a turn.
- Turn the outside ski intentionally into the fall line, in order to make the turn easier, meaning that you not only do the transition forward and force your ski into the new direction through tilting, turning or swinging your upper body around hard, but that the change of directions and the transition are a smooth and simultaneous action.

- Imagine you are a soccer player who wants to shoot a ball laying downhill and diagonally in front of you. The ball is not supposed to fly across the whole field, but should, as a precise and well timed shot, take it 10-15 meters away. If you shoot too powerfully, you fully extend your leg and this is something we are trying to avoid.
- Or you imagine to have a headlight mounted on your outside knee and try to shine it into the new direction as quickly as possible. This light only works as long as your knee is bent.
- Plant your pole before you do the transition.

Learn the dynamic transition by hopping explosively into the new direction

- For fast directional changes: Transition with an explosive vertical movement: to get the skis out of the snow and to do the directional change dynamically and with lots of power.

- Use the dynamics not vertically, but horizontally; put just as much power into the direction or the transition, but do it without hopping.
- Rhythmical sequence of several Telemark turns with a measured out power input.

Telemark turn with pole plant, transition and optimal body position

Just in case that one or the other Telemark pupil cannot keep up with the learning speed of the rest of the group, we still have the good old snow plow as a recommendable alternative, even though the methodical way working with a parallel ski position is due to the modern material, still the #1 choice for instructing beginners. Coming out of a traverse, the insecure novice therefore brings his skis into a plow position and initiates the turn.

After crossing the fall line, he lets the back foot slide back and finishes the turn in a Telemark position. After a few successful attempts, he should try to minimize the plow position and to push the inside ski back even earlier, until the snow plow finally disappears.

Telemark plow: Start in a Telemark position, get into a snow plow, initiate the turn and finish it in a Telemark position again

3.1.4 Step 4:
Improving the Telemark Turn Technique

We can now be a little proud of ourselves, since we are now able to ski down easy slopes with a light decline in the Telemark turn - but to impress the snowboarders and alpine skiers still passing us by, we need more exercise and now want to improve and consolidate our Telemark turn technique with step 4. Therefore we have to find a stable upper body position, support the rhythmical flow of the turns with our poles, gain more safety through the equal weighting of our skis, initiate the turn more effective with simple body movements, steer the turn with maximum edge control and react to different forms of terrain with different turn radii.

More speed, more dynamics

I. Upper Body

Old technique: Twisting or counter-rotating the upper body

The times when Telemarkers used to ski with an extremely twisted or in technical terms, counter-rotated, upper body, belong in the past. This position is on the one hand unhealthy, since the spinal column is loaded unfavorably and on the other hand it is very difficult to transfer enough power onto your skis in this position.

As a consequence, we are trying to find a posture for Telemarking which corresponds with our everyday motor activity. With a little fantasy, you can compare Telemarking with normal walking – you use big steps to walk down a hill, change the direction with every step and shift your weight constantly. While walking in a street it is completely normal for us that our posture is oriented in the direction of the movement – we are going where we are looking.

Telemarking simply follows the same principle of movement. According to this, both the body and mainly the head should face into the direction of travel: before, during and after the turn. It is not as simple as in the case of modern alpine carving, where the feet are in a parallel position, to get into this frontal position, though. Due to the step position the pelvis of the Telemarker is slightly turned towards the mountain which is compensated through a countermovement of the shoulder axis. The result is also a frontal position for Telemarking.

It is just as important that you are looking forward to where you are going and not down on your skis - same as the driver of a car, who doesn't stare at his hood or his steering wheel, but watches the traffic ahead.

With all this in mind, you not only have a position on your skis which is approved in everyday life, but you can use your upper body extremely effectively as well.

This stable position is supported by your arms, which are included in this posture – your hands with the poles are held with tension in front of your body and with slightly bent elbows. To consolidate this posture, it is important to ski without poles as often as possible, because then you have one thing less to concentrate on.

Frontal position of the upper body

What I can do
- Stringing together Telemark turns at a moderate speed and on a mellow grade.

What I want to learn
- Using the forces of the upper body effectively.
- The upper body points into the direction of travel in every phase of the turn.

What I have to do
- The shoulder axis compensates for the angle of the pelvis and therefore the body is standing at right angles to the direction of travel.
- The tip of your nose is pointing towards the tip of your skis.
- Your arms, with the poles, are held in front of the body.

How I can learn it
- Get back to the contrast exercises of step 2: Twist your upper body downhill, uphill and into the direction of travel. Doing this, you have to have a clock in mind: straight forward is 12 o'clock, to the left is 9 o'clock and to the right is 3 o'clock.

- Self control rides in a frontal position: Cross your poles behind your body, at hip height – if the tips of the poles always stay between the skis, you remain in frontal position.
- Hold your ski poles in the middle and keep them lateral to the skis – if they stay parallel to your skis, you remain in frontal position.
- Hold the poles in front of the body like a paddle – they have to remain in right angles to the skis.

Lurk/slalom pole in right angles to the ski

- Hold the poles in your neck and keep them in right angles to the direction of travel.
- Turn your poles upside down, with the tips pointing into the air – you should see your skis between your hands all the time.
- Hold your poles in right angles to the direction of travel on the tips of your index fingers.
- Ski without poles in a compact frontal position and keep your arms stretched out.

II. Weighting of the Skis

In this stage of the learning process it often is difficult for a Telemarking novice to weight both skis equally. The uphill ski mostly is dragged behind the leading, outside ski and has no weight load at all. The result is a pretty insecure and unstable position, which only looks like a tele-turn, but has to be carried out like a poor alpine turn, due to the missing load on the inside ski. In the following learning sequence, we are trying to get a feeling for the optimum weight distribution on both skis.

Equally weighted skis

It does not really matter whether the weight distribution on both skis is 50:50 – the only thing that really counts is to put enough weight on your uphill ski to be able to stand on both feet safely. This is the one and only precondition for really radical and extreme skiing, one day to come.

Once you work with two skis and two edges you not only have a better balance and more control, but then you can really lean into a turn. In addition, you can really push your uphill ski dynamically forward as soon as it is weighted actively.

Since most of us are not having too many problems with the leading or the outside ski, the main thing in the following exercises will be the inside or the tracking ski.

What I can do
- Stringing together Telemark turns.
- Frontal body position.

What I want to learn
- Putting weight on the uphill ski.
- Conditionally putting weight on either ski.

What I have to do
- Stand on your whole forefoot and not only on the tips of your toes if you put weight on your uphill ski.
- Pull your back leg right underneath your butt.
- Find a neutral position for your body, with the slight tendency to take your upper body back.
- Put weight on the whole sole of your front foot, with the tendency to put more weight on your heel.

How I can learn it
- Contrast exercise: Ski only on the downhill, or the uphill ski, and on both skis together.

Ski on your uphill ski, lifting your downhill ski up

- Improve the equal weighting of the skis: Lift your downhill ski while skiing across the fall line.
- Squeeze a bug, which is located between the sole and the binding, with the ball of your back foot.
- Put the whole weight before, during and after the turn, mentally on the uphill ski.

- Try to come to a stop with the back ski and try to pile up as much snow as possible.
- Do a "Fakie" – that means to do a Telemark turn the other way round. Through this the back ski is the downhill ski and the novice learns to put weight on the "bent" leg.

Fakie

- Ski without a transition – that means that you have to remain in the position that you once have taken, throughout the whole ride. Keep your weight load on the downhill ski and on the uphill ski, no matter in which direction you are going.
- Take your upper body slightly back while skiing, to move your weight load backward (heel of the front foot, ball of the back foot).

Telemark turning without a transition

The upper body is taken backward, in order to intensify the load on the back leg

III. The Pole Plant

When Sondre NORHEIM demonstrated the first turns in Telemark technique in 1860 in Norway, a pole or its use still was completely strange for him. Only a few years later, the skiers in Norway realized that a long wooden pole was very helpful, not only for walking, but also for skiing. If they were moving on even ground they had the poles to push themselves off and for going downhill they were a good means to keep the balance and to do safer turns.

Starting out in Lapland, the two pole technique gained acceptance at the beginning of the 20th century. With two poles one could repel better in cross-country skiing and they offered more stability for downhill skiing, since the upper body was held steadier and it was easier to carry out an exact timing for the turns.

Today there are a lot of Telemarkers who still ski with this long wooden pole, called a lurk, in memory of the old times, using it on the inside of long turns like an outrigger. This way of skiing does not only look pretty spectacular, but is big time fun and as well trains the right lean to the inside of the turn. Every Telemarker should therefore try this super cool way of shredding, from time to time.

Our aim, however, is to ski with two poles and to use them as effectively as possible. For the first attempts in Telemark skiing the poles are used primarily to support the balance. For an advanced Telemarker the poles mainly give the initiation for a turn – the pole plant therefore is on the one hand an aid to find a turning rhythm and on the other, it makes the upper body turn into the center of the turn, which is exactly the direction of the turning skis.

The way poles are used depends on the speed and the radius of the turn (short or wide turns). For a short turn, which is skied with less speed, it is carried out powerfully between tip and binding of the front or leading ski.

For big turns with little speed, the pole plant is carried out in the front third of the ski, as for turns with high speeds, the poles aren't used at all, or their use only is indicated. If they were namely used with a lot of power, the upper body gets an intense counter movement and the optimal, compact position disappears.

For short turns the pole plant is closer to boot and binding

For wide turns with a high speed the pole plant is no longer necessary

What I can do
- Stringing together Telemark turns.
- Frontal body position.
- Weight skis equally.

What I want to learn
- Pole plant as initiation for a turn.

What I have to do
- Bring the downhill arm forward during the traverse, without stretching it out completely. Slightly bend your elbow and push the tip of the pole into the snow.
- The pole plant is carried out between binding and ski tip on the downhill side.

How I can learn it
- Ski with one long pole.
- Contrast exercise with two poles: at one time you only plant the uphill pole on the outside of the turn, at the other, you plant the downhill pole on the inside of the turn.
- Plant both poles first on the uphill and then on the downhill side.
- Ski with a double pole plant.

- Practice the timing for the pole plant in the traverse (without doing a turn).
- Get a yelled command from your partner for the pole plant and the turn initiation.
- Doing turns with an appropriate pole plant.

Powerful pole plant

IV. Turn Initiation

The most important prerequisite to do a Telemark turn is the dynamic transition into the new direction of travel. This turn initiation is supported, or even made easier, by a corresponding movement of the upper body. This movement can be carried out in two ways: By a prerotation of the upper body into the new direction, or by tilting the whole body into the center of the turn.

As already described, the hip axis of a Telemarker is lined up to the mountain. This means that his way from the traverse into the fall line is longer. This fact often causes problems for beginners and even advanced skiers, because they are not able to overcome this distance. A good approach to eliminate this handicap is to simultaneously with the pole plant, prerotate the upper body slightly downhill and into the new direction of travel. With that, the long distance is outwitted and the skis follow the movement that the upper body already has executed.

The body proceeds like a winded up spring, because through the prerotation, a tension has been built up between the body and the legs, which now can be dissolved and used for the initiation of the turn. If the upper body rotates downhill, the skis are held flat. Only in the fall line do the skis change the edges and the turn can finally be steered out.

Turn initiation with a tilt   *Turn initiation with prerotation*

The far more sporty solution consists, however, in tilting the body into the center of the turn. The upper body, which takes a tighter and more direct line than the skis with this technique, is tilted over the skis into the center of the turn, facing downhill. Only in the last moment do the skis get back under the body and catch it.

This technique requires more courage of the skier than the prerotation, since he really throws his upper body downhill – but this technique ensures a quick turn initiation, a good tracking of the edges and an optimal turn control.

As a good Telemarker, you should be able to master both versions of the turn initiation. Depending on speed, terrain and other outer conditions, both tilting and rotating are similarly important.

What I can do
- A series of Telemark turns.
- Frontal body position.
- Pole plant for the turn initiation.
- Weight skis equally.

What I want to learn
- Optimize the turn initiation with the prerotation of the upper body or the tilting of the whole body.

What I have to do
- Prerotation: Simultaneous with the pole plant, the upper body turns intentionally into the new direction of travel; upper body and legs are not pointing in the same direction for a short instance; through this, tension is built up and the skis turn more easily in the direction indicated by the upper body.
- Tilting: Simultaneous with the pole plant the whole body is tilted downhill, over the skis; body and skis are on different tracks; only at the end of the turn the skis come back under the body and catch it..

How I can learn it

Prerotation

- Golfer turn: Both poles are held together; for the turn initiation you take a big swing uphill with the poles and let the stroke sweep across the skis to the other side.
- Boxer turn: This turn is initiated by a tremendous punch with the hand on the outside of the turn.
- Welcome turn: You welcome an imaginary friend with your uphill hand on the down hill side.

Prerotation with a welcome turn

- Hitchhiker turn: In the traverse you take the thumb of your downhill hand up and downhill; if your shoulder follows this motion with a twist, you succeed.
- Waiter turn: The poles are held like a tray in front of your body, on the downhill side this tray with filled glasses is served to a guest.
- Corkscrew turn: Your head is the corkscrew which pulls the cork out of the bottle; thus the head turns into the turn first, than the shoulders, than upper body and skis.

Tilting

- Couch potato turn: Do a turn without any active turning mechanisms – the skis turn only through the edging.
- Airplane turn: Ski without poles and spread your arms like wings – the turn is initiated through the tilting of the spread out arms, to the downhill side.
- Paddle turn: A long pole is held in front of the body. For the initiation of the turn, the paddle is tilted downhill and "falls" into the center of the turn.

Tilting with a paddle turn

- Gripping the stars-turn: With your uphill hand you try to grab some stars above your head and on the downhill side – again your body "falls" downhill and the turn is initiated.
- Motorcycle turn: The poles are held like a bike handlebar across the direction of travel – to initiate the turn, you steer into it, like a bike rider. Thus your body prerotates slightly and is tilted into the center at the same time.

V. Steering a Turn

As important as the initiation of the turn is the steering of it, once you have crossed the fall line - namely we are not aiming to skid down the slope with zero control, but instead we want to finish each turn securely and neatly. To reach this goal, there are a couple of simple tricks. Of course out of all the things that we have learned already, the following are a prerequisite: equal weight on both skis, frontal body position, wide stance.

Our attention is directed to our feet and legs first. With their help we can make sure that the skis are not remaining in a flat position. Because if the skis are in the snow with their whole base, the only thing that they can do is skid. As a consequence the turn is carried out with very little control.

Equal weight on both skis, frontal body position, wide stance

We rather want to achieve that the skis are edged properly. Only then are you able to steer a turn exactly. For this you have to tilt your feet to the side of the big toe (downhill ski) and to the side of the little toe (uphill ski). As an additional effect you achieve that the skis get a resistance in the snow and that the edges bite well – and this makes it easier to initiate the next turn, since you avoid an insecure sliding phase at the end it.

The pressure of the edges can be improved with a perfect interaction between them and the upper body. Either the body is tilted into the center of the turn in a stretched position (stretched turn position), so that its forces have a direct effect on the edges via the legs and the feet – or you bend your hip (bent turn position) and push your hip together with your knees uphill, to improve the pressure on your edges by this.

Pushing the hips and knees uphill is compensated by a counter movement of the upper body. The result is called, according to its looks and it's shape: The banana edge.

Both in the stretched as well as in the bent turn position, you should take care of a wide stance (a least a hands width between the two boards) and an equal load on both skis to maximize the edging.

What I can
- Series of Telemark turns.
- Turn initiation through tilt and rotation.
- Equal weight distribution.
- Frontal body position.

What I want to learn
- Finishing and steering a turn with maximum edge control.
- Wide stance.

What I have to do
- Do not weight the whole sole of your foot, but the side of your big toe on your downhill ski and the side of your little toe on your uphill ski.

- The whole body is tilted into the center of the turn.
- Both hip and knees are pushed uphill.

How I can learn it
- Ski with open boots.
- Put your skis flat in the snow and then edge them by putting weight on your little and your big toe – let a second person stand on your side to grab you, in case you fall over.

Flat skis and edged skis

- Same exercise as before: This time you are on a slope standing across the fall line – feel the difference between a flat and an edged ski – sliding, braking.
- Try the same while doing a traverse – slide, edge, slide. Try to "cut the slope open" with your edges and feel the difference between the different leans and angles of your hip and your knees.
- Do an uphill christie in Telemark position and check your tracks in the snow – you should see two of them!

- Breake turn: Let the flat skis skid a little after the turn initiation, count to three and then edge them.
- Edge the skis in a turn by putting load on your big toe- and your little toe side
- Improve the pressure on your edges by pushing your knees uphill: push both knees towards your inside hand with the step turn.
- Improve the pressure on your edges by pushing your hip uphill: Imagine you are squeezing an apple in your downhill hip. The apple gets kicked out for the turn initiation and squeezed in again on the new downhill side.
- Speed up at the end of the base training; through higher speeds you gain not only safety but also self-confidence and courage.

Hips and knees are pushing uphill, skis on the edges (banana edge)

3.2 Action and Fun

Now we are doing turns on a pretty high level, but of course it doesn't reach yet for the best thirty of a Telemark race. We are still missing the dynamics and the speed, which gives our skiing the extra something. Once we have found this extra something, Telemarking turns into ecstasy. Then it doesn't play a role anymore what the weather is like – we are out skiing, even in the worst conditions and the only thing that counts is the Telemark addiction. From now on you experience feelings by simply doing a turn that you never would have dreamed of on alpine boards and with a fixed heel. Carving a groomed slope, ripping the moguls, doing air in the half pipe and phat lines in the powder – alpine skiing and boarding rocks, but Telemark rules.

If it were easy it'd be called snowboarding – a Telemarker, taking some air in the halfpipe

3.2.1 Carving

Carving – the magic word that has ruled the winter world for a couple of years. Also, or especially for the Telemarkers, carving has it's fascination and it really works! Luckily, there are no complicated techniques and long learning processes required to carve on your tele-boards. It only takes a slight edging and a little tilt of your body into the center of the turn to make the skis turn almost by themselves. Because this is our main goal if we are telecarving: right from the beginning the turn is initiated and steered along the side-cut of the ski. The edges are not supposed to skid diagonally across the snow, but cut, or carve, across it. The main prerequisite for this, is of course a ski with a deep side-cut, a raiser plate underneath the binding and a pretty stiff plastic boot.

In the 19th century, Sondre NORHEIM used to carve waists into his skis, to make use of the effect of a ski with a side-cut, which is said to have been 15 mm at this time. Definitely not enough to do any radical turns, but sufficient for changing the direction easier and faster than on straight boards.

Skiing like on railroad tracks: a carving Telemarker

Just like an airplane, which needs a certain speed for the take off, we have to have a high enough speed to get the maximum fun. But to be able to handle a higher speed sovereign and relaxed, we have to have maximum control first: Your body and your skis must work together a hundred percent.

The body is held in a frontal position and your arms are bent at height of the belly. This position allows a direct and optimal transfer of power between body and ski, making it possible to steer the turn along the edges right after the turn initiation – because this is the decisive effect: All actions have to be finished before the actual turn. For the Telemarker this means that the transition, change of the edges and the position, have to be carried out early enough.

If you do the transition, it is important that the outside ski is not pushed in the direction of the fall line, but forward. You also have to tilt your body into the center of the turn, before the change of direction. Only this tilt allows your skis to change the edges in the stage of the turn initiation. This "falling into the turn", should be done towards the end of the skis, because thus they get loaded and the Telemark position is stabilized. If these actions are carried out right, you can ski along the side-cut of your teles as if you were on railroad tracks.

Doing carved turns gives your legs another special duty. A deep and very static Telemark position obstructs a flexible style of skiing. We rather have to learn to bend and to stretch our legs in order to build up or to release pressure if needed. Thus the legs are used as shock absorbers. In the beginning of the steering phase the ski has to be edged, so it does not slide anymore, but carve – don't engage the edges too hard, because then you loose too much speed.

At the end of the steering phase you relax your legs and go down into a deeper position in order to absorb the resulting pressure with the help of centrifugal force and gravity. To initiate the next turn, you go back to a tall stance, without starting to turn your skis again, because then it gets very hard to make the edges bite again.

What I can do

- Weight skis equally.
- Frontal position.
- Tilt for turn initiation.
- Finish the steering phase of the turn on the edges.
- Wide stance.

What I want to learn

- Do the transition, the change of the edge and the position before the change of direction.
- Do a turn along the skis side-cut right from the beginning.
- Tilt to the tails of the skis.
- Handle a high speed.

What I have to do

- -At first the transition is carried out: The uphill ski is pushed forward and the downhill ski back.
- Tilt into the center of the turn with your hip and your upper body.
- Simultaneously with the tilt, the edges are changed.
- The turn is finished along the side-cut of the skis in Telemark position.
- The body faces into the direction of travel all the time – it may not be twisted into or against the direction of travel.

How I can learn it

- Feel the carving effect of the skis in an alpine position through tilting your body, or only by rolling the soles of your feet.
- Start carving again in an alpine position, but as soon as you cross the fall line, you go down into the Telemark position and finish the turn along the side-cut of your skis.

Tilt to the tails of the skis

The tip of the downhill ski can take off

- Do the transition before the change of direction, change the edges and the position and then initiate and finish the turn in Telemark position along the side-cut of the skis.
- Tilt to the tails of your skis (there it can even happen that the tip of your downhill ski is taking off).
- Do turns without a vertical movement.
- Intensify the carving effect by taking the front knee back – thus the ski gets a better edging.

The edging of the skis becomes more effective if you do not push the front leg too far forward, but take it further back

- You can support a quick change of edges and position by doing a racing dive turn (you sorta racing dive downhill after the step turn) or a wipe turn (you quickly wipe a table clean with both hands from the uphill to the downhill side).
- To improve the lean into the turn you have the following exercises to choose from: Outrigger (the outside arm is dragging into the turn, the inside arm is stretched out in a right angle from the body into the snow to the center of the turn like an outrigger), Snowcarver (Who succeeds to touch the snow in an upright position and a stretched out inside arm?).

3.2.2 The Short Turn

With the carved turns you now can handle flat and neatly groomed pistes pretty well – and even get the looks from fellow skiers more and more often. But the real challenges are found in different terrain: steep and icy mogul runs and deep snow. But for a decent show off under such conditions, you are supposed to have a real idea of the short turn and it's application.

For this technique the legs decide for a good performance, then the upper body – they have to work really quickly and dynamically for the short turn. But also other movements, like the pole plant are carried out with a lot of power. The poles have much more meaning for short as for carved turns. They serve as a rhythm stabilizer and if used perfectly, they already provide the turn radii so to say.

Short turn: dynamic step change and compact upper body

The whole posture at the short turn is small and compact and should be kept like this, if possible, during the whole turn. This means that there is no vertical movement carried out. Protruding movements last too long and therefore, work against a quick initiation, turning and steering of the short turn. The step mustn't be too long either, since otherwise, the way from one turn to the other, is far too long. At carved short turns the upper body is taken along into the new direction of travel to apply the edges with the most optimal transmission of power possible. Before a new change of direction, the upper body is slightly counter-rotated in order to shorten the way into the next turn. For extremely short turns, as we need them in steep and narrow terrain, or later on, in mogul runs, the upper body always is aligned downhill. Through this, we can react even faster and raise the frequency of our turns, since only our legs "work". Therefore, one talks of short turning as leg-oriented skiing, while carving is more body oriented.

Slight counter-rotation of the upper body

What I can do
- Weight the skis equally.
- Pole Plant.
- Finish a turn on the edges.

What I want to learn
- Short and dynamic pole plant.
- Short and dynamic transition.
- Hands at belly height in front of the body.
- Quick turning of the legs to the inside of the turn.
- Quiet upper body.
- Depending on the turn frequency: take the upper body along into the turn and "open" its position at the end of the turn or constantly align the upper body downhill.
- Extreme and short edging of the skis.
- Rhythmical sequences of turns with short radii.
- Low and compact body position.

What I have to do
- Dynamic pole plant.
- Aggressive and extreme edging of the skis, to gain a decelerating effect and a vertical rebound of the body.
- Turn your skis almost at right angles to the fall line.
- Use the counter movement to decelerate and to do a fast transition, or to turn the skis into the new direction of travel.
- Rhythmical and controlled skiing with short turns.

How I can learn it
- Practice a quick and dynamic transition, going straight down or in a traverse, with a pole plant and without changing directions.
- Ski in the fall line in flat terrain, slightly twist your upper body in both directions and find a rhythm for this.
- Shorten the turn radii (from mid size to short).
- Take your inside ski back, really intentionally.
- Hockey stop: Quick and aggressive deceleration to a stand still.

- Breathe consciously with every turn.
- Short turn in a corridor: First without a pole plant, while keeping your poles upside down like candles, then with a proper holding of the poles, without a pole plant, finally with a proper pole plant.
- Partner exercise: Ski synchronized with rhythm changes, get your rhythm through acoustical commands, follow and keep a better Telemarker's tracks, ski next to a better Telemarker.
- Aggressive short turning with a distinct vertical movement (you can even jump for this), to practice a quick and dynamic step change.
- Short turns in a stable and low position (you have snow contact all the time) without a vertical movement – all the dynamics are in the step change.
- Short turns in steep terrain.

Deep position and extreme pole plant

If you are doing a good job in the moguls you are also the boss in any other terrain

3.2.3 Mogul Skiing

For some Telemarkers, moguls are little, nasty monsters that are only there to give them a bad time anytime they come their way. But the moguls that we are talking about in this chapter are also deeply loved by a lot of free-heelers, because skiing in a terrain which is as kicky as selective means a big challenge. Once you are into it, you don't want to miss them anymore.

Nevertheless there is no mogul run like the other – and that's what it's all about. The one time you cut straight through, the next time you fly right over – and everything is different to the run that you have done only a few minutes ago.

The only thing that counts is that you don't let the "nasty mogulz" scare you – try to let them work for and not against you. Find a technique and a line that allows you to string turns and jumps together in your own rhythm – just go and rock 'em.

To be able to handle the changing terrain well or even perfectly, we do not need completely new skiing skills. We can use the now well-practiced short turn and only have to combine it with a special absorbing technique that helps us to keep snow contact and avoids a dressing down.

We therefore use our legs like shock absorbers, meaning that we can level out moguls and bumps by only bending and stretching our legs. As long as we don't want to do stunts like helicopters and flips, this permanent snow contact is an important prerequisite to ski a good and safe line in a mogul run.

Losing permanent snow contact unintentionally means that you go out of control and take up more and more speed – there are no brakes once you are air-bound. As long as we ski with permanent snow contact through the moguls, we are able to control our speed with dynamic edging and to turn the skis out of the fall line.

You sure need a certain minimum speed to keep your movements and turns fluent – but don't mistake this minimum speed with crashing down through the moguls and the run.

However, success or failure is not only guaranteed by the shock absorbing function of your legs. There are quite a few other things which have to be taken into the account, if you really want to have fun in the mogul runs. First of all, you are supposed to have a really tight stance on your boards, to achieve something called "forming a block". This block helps you to weight your skis equally and synchronizes the dynamic edging and deceleration. Besides, there hardly is enough space between the single moguls to have a wide stance. As a result you would ski on two different levels and would not be able to act and react in a direct and well-aimed motion.

 So that the legs can work effectively, the upper body may not transfer any superficial movements. This means that mainly the trunk, but also the arms, are not working against the overall movement during these fast and short actions.

Always try to have equal load on your skis in every phase of the turn

As a consequence, you always keep your arms in front of your upper body and in your field of vision – only then can they respond with a quick and dynamic pole plant, which is carried out close to the front foot for a short radius turn. If you plant your pole closer to the ski tip, the resulting turn would be too wide and is not suited for the fast action in the moguls. Beware after each pole plant that the hand with the pole does not go back behind your hip on the inside. This leads to a upper body rotation which goes way too far, it cannot follow the quick movements of the legs anymore and you get into a back lean position.

But also your trunk contributes its part for your safe ride through the moguls. It always should be held in a neutral position – once you have too much forward lean, you limit your mobility for the absorbtion of the moguls drastically. It is same with too much back lean – once you leave the neutral middle position and start "sitting" on your tails, you lose control and get thrown off, like a bull rider.

Same as a forward or back lean, you should try to avoid a frontal position. If you rotate your upper body into the direction of travel with every turn, it takes way too long to be ready for the next one. Therefore we are trying to always align our upper body downhill as long as we are in the moguls – the distances are less and you can react much more quickly.

If you do a pole plant, your downhill arm should be taken in slightly and your uphill arm or shoulder, distinctively forward – your upper body thus is "open" , prerotated to the downhill side and makes it easier for the skis to turn in the fall line. Because this is what we are looking for: skiing a direct line and trying to avoid long and boring traverses. Finally, we're skiing moguls and not cross-country.

Another challenge is the fact that every mogul run has a profile of it's own. One time the moguls and hollows are more distinctive, the other time the distances are irregular. Even if you choose a line only 5 meters next to your previous one, both the situation and the rhythm can already be totally different. For us this means that we have to handle new situations with every run. To master these conditions, we always have to ski with a look ahead, meaning that we constantly have to visualize situations expecting us 2 or 3 moguls further.

There are three different ways to choose your line. The easiest one goes right across the moguls – in this case you turn your skis on top of the moguls, where you have the least snow resistance. Certainly, we have to bend and stretch our legs really actively along this track, since here we have the biggest motion amplitudes. A second option is to ski the line around the moguls.

You don't go to the top, but stay in the hollows – not suited for bigger jumps, but it sure is a fast and straight line. The third variant – the line through the moguls – definitely is the most radical and sporty. In this case we are not turning across the moguls or in the deep hollows, but run into the mogul in its upper third. This is a very direct line on which you have to react quickly and radically to keep control, but finally it still is the terrain which gives you the line to ski on.

A track across the moguls (left), around the moguls (center) and through the moguls (right)

What I can do

- Weight skis equally.
- Narrow stance.
- Quick turning.
- Short turns in the fall line.
- Rhythmical and dynamic pole plant.
- Edge the skis aggressively.

What I want to learn

- Absorbing technique (bending and stretching the legs).
- Active crouching, mainly for big moguls.
- Aligning the upper body downhill.
- Variable skiing technique to compensate for impaired balance and technical mistakes.
- Subordinate to the rhythm of the moguls and use the moguls and hollows for a own line.

What I have to do

- Always keep contact to the snow.
- Always keep your arms in front of you.
- Upper body is centered, to keep balance and be ready to react.
- Upper body is aligned downhill.
- Narrow stance.
- Rhythmical and dynamic pole plant.
- Bend your legs before you go across the mogul.
- The upper body turns downhill, pole plant is carried out simultaneously.
- Do the transition on the mogul and the turn initiation in the fall line.

The upper body is aligned downhill

- Stretch your legs into the hollow after crossing the mogul and try to use the "discharge", given by the terrain to turn your skis further – decelerate if you are going down the mogul.
- Decelerate through edging slightly and bringing your skis across the fall line after you are through the hollow between two moguls – your upper body remains aligned downhill.

How I can learn it

- Practice the short turn on a shallow slope in a deep position and without a vertical movement.
- Practice the short turn on a normal slope, do a turn with a down unweighting to imitate the absorbing technique.
- Rhythm exercises for the short turn on a normal slope (see also chapter 3.2.2 "The short turn").
- Practice your pole plant (see also chapter 3.2.2 "The short turn").
- If available: Ski through wave sections – first absorb the waves with your legs (meaning let the terrain bend your legs), then go actively down on top of the wave and stretch again in the trough.
- Traverse in the moguls with and without poles, get used to the bumps and the uneven shape of the slope – bend your legs on top, stretch them in the trough, but beware the back lean!
- Face your fears and accelerate in the traverse or start jumping the moguls.
- Do a standing exercise to internalize the basic position.
- Practice the basic move on one mogul again and again.
- Always go across the moguls in the beginning.

Learn to find a good line by spooning a better skier

- First do three turns in a row in the mogul run.
- Follow a good skier right behind and learn to find a good line, where to initiate turns and where to finish them.
- Look for a given line and try to stick to it – now you don't ski across, but finally through the moguls.

Powder – the deeper, the better

3.2.4 Deep Snow

It is addictive, it blows your mind, it gives you an endorphin fallout, enough for the next two weeks – powder snow. Is there anything better out there, than a phat Telemark turn in fresh, spraying snow? This is a high which is hard to describe. Just have a look into a Telemarkers eyes after a perfect powder day – no more words required.

Ever since the time of Sondre NORHEIM, deep snow skiing has been the magic word for all ski freaks. The folks in Morgedal had no idea of groomed slopes – being the first freeriders and ski bums in ski history, they skied everything in any snow all over the mountain.

For us modern Telemarkers the "white gold" is still doping for our souls. We can enjoy these magic moments still more intensively in a deep step position and are a lot closer to the snow due to the Telemark position Moreover, this harmonic movement of the transition goes along awesome with the floating in deep snow. Telemarkers are flying down the runs, apparently without a solid ground, stringing almost effortlessly one turn into the other while having this permanent and "mean" glimmer in their eyes.

Everybody who has tried it wants to do it again and is ready to give a few things for this white high – sometimes thoughtlessly disregarding all the possible risks.

Pretty often this can be a fatal mistake. A mountain changes its look daily and avalanches kill way too many people every year. So be prepared and take a few lifesaving measures before you go for the white rush.

Never ski deep snow on your own, check the local avalanche forecast, and be prepared for a possible avalanche by means of your personal equipment. Always carry a shovel, a probe and an avalanche transceiver, if you are out there in the ungroomed. Safety first! Only if you are able to evaluate alpine dangers and if you are technically prepared for the case of emergency, may you throw yourself into the incomparable pleasure of deep snow skiing.

Simply a dream: untouched powder runs

But the Telemark gods have put practicing before the weightless high in deep snow. Skiing in deep snow namely takes you into a dimension that you have not experienced on a groomed slope, where you have to orientate yourself mainly in the two-dimensional space. The snow is hardpacked and you move mainly forward and backward and to the sides. This gets different once you are in the powder. You sink into it and experience a third dimension, the vertical orientation – a feeling as if you would float or fly (...probably the main reason, why so many Telemarkers are in love with the deep snow!). At the same time, this third dimension at first can be a real problem for the inexperienced.

Along with the right equipment and a proper technique, it does not take too long to learn everything about this 3-D fascination and to enjoy it thereafter. Beyond all doubts, it is a lot easier to ski deep snow on wider and softer skis and even if you don't have real free ride skis, right from the start you are doing fine with all-around carvers which are not too short. The wider the boards, the more flotation they provide, is the simple rule.

Falls in the deep snow are nothing special for Telemarkers

It is of similar advantage if you use softer skis in the deep snow, because they turn easier, even at low speeds. On a groomed slope of course you are facing the fact that soft skis are not performing as quiet as stiffer ones, since the edges do not have the aggressive bite which is required for hardpacked snow and ice – but for skiing powder you actually don't need edges at all. Both skis are rather gliding on their whole base. Important again: distribute your weight equally and load uphill and downhill ski for more flotation.

This "standing on both skis" is also of great importance for the turn initiation in the deep snow, because only then can you use two boards at the same time as a safe "platform". The compression of the snow of course is optimal if you have a narrow stance, because this also keeps the skis from sinking deeply into the snow. All these single components together with a Telemark transition are leading to a sweet and lovely rebound effect – you lower your center of gravity, compress the snow, get pushed back up and can now easily turn your unweighted skis, despite the higher snow resistance.

Nevertheless, the most decisive factor for maximum fun, still is the right position. To provide your skis from digging into the snow, it is essential to have only very little pressure on your tips. Shift your weight backwards, ski your boards with increased pressure on their tails and try to keep your tips as far as possible to the snow surface, or above it.

Another important factor in deep-snow-fun-calculation are the poles. If the baskets that you are using are too small, your powder performance drops below zero within a few seconds. This is because the poles are sinking to deep into the snow and cannot provide you with the required resistance for an optimal position. Solution: Mount bigger baskets and increase the efficiency of your poles by a hundred percent.

Another piece of equipment that you can leave at home with husband/wife and children is your cool Norwegian sweater – no such thing required on a powder day. Even without a fall you will be soaking wet after a few runs, from the spraying snow alone. Wear functional water- and windproof ski or mountain clothing and even a head first dive into the white stuff isn't a real threat anymore. Next thing to have in mind – switch your sunglasses for goggles. They give you excellent protection and vision and opposite to your sunglasses, it takes a real crash to lose them. Talking about crashes: A-l-w-a-y-s wear knee pads if you are going off-piste!

They sell for a much more affordable price than a surgical reconstruction of your patella and last but not least, look twice as cool as the Norwegian wool that you have left in your closet. Another thing which really has cool looks and gives you

Be quiet and enjoy – this is what deep snow skiing is all about

maximum protection in the ungroomed and steep is a ski helmet. Better wear it two times too often, than one time too less. Together with the above mentioned standard safety equipment, you are now ready to take off.

Skiing in deep snow does technically not differ too much from your turns on groomed slopes; you simply have to learn that your skis do the job. Try to find the "platform" as described above and make use of your skis' rebound effect. As long as the powder snow is not higher than 30-40 cm, we can go back to the already familiar movements of on-piste Telemarking. The turn is initiated by a tilt into the center of the turn and a slight prerotation into the new direction of travel. To finish a turn, you use both your equally weighted skis, as usual. This means that the transition is carried out almost without any vertical movement.

No need to beam me up, Scotty. Nirvana found.

The situation changes if you are confronted with breaking crust snow, real deep powder or wet fresh snow. Then there is only one recipe that helps you to survive: lift your legs up and turn your skis into the new direction with an extreme vertical movement. You can use your outside arm as an additional help in these heavy snow conditions as well. If you take it into the new direction with a sweep, together with the transition and the vertical movement, you are able to do good and sovereign turns even under difficult conditions.

Decisive for a sovereign style in the deep snow, is also an adequate speed. Speed does not only provide you with an impressive appearance, but helps you with every single turn. The more forward momentum you have, the easier it is to overcome the higher snow resistance in deep snow.

For us this means: short turns, pretty fast, close to the fall line. To be able to stay as close as possible to the fall line we need to move quickly and fluently. A good pole plant also is very important: It gives you rhythm and your body gets back into the right position with every turn.

In conclusion we can say that you have to ski far more sensitively in deep snow than on groomed terrain. The snow conditions can change within seconds – you are just flying through knee deep powder, when five meters later a strip of windpacked snow stops you and turns you upside down.

No friends on powder days

What I can do
- Short turn.
- Equal weight on both skis.
- Pole plant.
- Dynamic turn initiation and a fast rotation.
- Compact position of the body.
- Narrow stance.
- Short turns in the fall line.

What I want to learn
- Skiing in a third dimension.
- Do a turn "out of the backside".
- Finish a turn on flat skis.
- Develop the feeling not to stand on two, but on one, big and wide ski, which cannot sink into the snow.
- No fear of speed.
- Ski also in deep snow dynamically in the fall line.
- Do an explosive up-unweighting, or compression, for the turn initiation in "thick" snow and braking crust snow.

No fear of speed in the deep snow   *Deep position*

What I have to do
- Relaxed posture.
- Deep position and at the same time an upright upper body.

- Ski close to the fall line to gain a higher basic speed.
- Narrow stance.
- Equally distributed weight.
- Overcome the higher snow resistance with higher speed and more muscle power.
- Avoid uncontrolled movements with your body and sudden load changes.

Light deep snow

- In light deep snow it is pretty easy, to apply the already learned technique of short turning, without any problems. Ski your turns not on the edges, but on the whole base of your skis; no normal position in the middle, but your body has to be backward and on the tails of your skis.

Body is slightly taken backward

- Crouch your legs during the transition and turn your skis over the fall line underneath your body.
- After this, your skis are gaining pressure again, the snow is getting compressed underneath your skis, and a rebound for the next turn is possible without too much effort.

Thick deep snow/breaking crust snow

- Deep body position at the beginning of the turn.
- Together with the pole plant you prerotate your upper body in the new direction.

Body slightly prerotated

- Explosive push off, or compression, with both legs, where the pole is used as a support.
- As soon as your thighs are brought up, do a transition in the air without snow contact.
- Turn over the fall line in the air and straighten up, or decompress, your whole body a little bit.
- Bend your legs strongly for the landing and let your body go back into a compact and deep position to get ready for the next turn.

How I can learn it

- Short turns (with and without a distinctive vertical movement) on a flat and groomed slope.
- Long traverses and straight down runs in ungroomed terrain, to get used to the deep snow and to find the right position; try a transition without changing the direction after a few training runs.
- Go straight down in the deep snow and do a uphill christie in Telemark position.
- Do a series of Telemark turns on mellow graded slope with a slight deep snow coverage.
- Ski next to a good track in the deep snow and try to repeat it.

Ski as close to the fall line as possible

- Ski next to a good Telemarker in the deep snow and try to take up the same rhythm.
- Imagine that you are a dolphin, which jumps out of the water with every transition, turns in the air and than dives back into the snow.
- Take your outside arm dynamically into the new direction.
- Plant your pole intentionally.
- For the sake of self control: Check your tracks after a run in the deep snow – check whether the pole plant has been carried out constantly, check whether your turns come regularly or whether you have a "chocolate side", whether you finish your turns or interrupt them early, whether you ski in the fall line or do too much traversing (do you ski your lines in a S- or in Z-shape?).
- Maximize speed, steepness and snow deepness in the course of time.

3.2.5 Ski Touring (Randonée = French for can't tele)

Why always ski on lift-served and groomed terrain? Sometimes every Telemarker gets caught by the desire to ski away from the prepared slopes. Standing in lift lines, pistes packed with other skiers and snowboarders and the skidding down on slopes which are as flat and wide as an Autobahn, gets dead boring after a certain time. As a consequence, more and more Telemarkers are going for the challenge of the remote backcountry, to climb mountains and peaks and to ski just like their forefathers.

Crowded pistes turn more and more Telemarkers into ski touring mountaineers

You might feel small and weak if you do your first tracks in this unique winter world of snow and rocks. But with every tour and almost every step, you get to like the silence and the seclusion more and finally find confidence in the mountains surrounding you. Any Telemarker who has had this intoxicating feeling which rewards you, once you have made it to the top, can understand, why ski touring can become a life long passion.

Even the ascent can be a particular natural experience

Well, it sure is not child's play to climb up a snow mountain on your own. But once you have found your personal rhythm, every step, which actually costs power and effort, turns out to be a unique experience anyway. Not to talk about the bliss you feel, if you reach the summit with hundreds and hundreds of vertical meters of powder or spring snow ahead of you.

So that the winter fairy tale becomes reality and does not turn into a nightmare, there are some important conditions and precautions that have to be considered. The adventure of ski touring is a heavenly pleasure only for those who can evaluate the particular dangers of winter mountaineering. You have to be able to judge your own skills as well as your personal shape and last but not least the omnipresent risk of avalanches, which are so dangerous and life-threatening, because they are invisible.

"No risk, no fun!" is a popular saying not only among the snowboarders. The Swiss "avalanche-pope" Werner Munter replies to that: "No limit, no life!"

For this reason every Telemarker should focus on the safety aspect of every tour first. You can reduce the risk by responsible preparation and circumspect behavior, to an acceptable minimum at every step, in the untouched nature. Being a good Telemark skier does not necessarily mean to be also a good ski mountaineer. Best thing is to do your first steps in the wilderness together with a mountain guide, or some experienced friends and to have in mind that ski touring also requires specialized equipment.

In steep or rocky sections of the ascent you have to take your skis off

First of all a touring ski should be lightweight – you save a lot of power in the ascent and second you have boards that turn easily, even in crust and wet snow, in the descent. Adjustable touring poles have the advantage that you can switch between a length that supports your climb and a length that is suited for skiing. Before the new 7tm release binding was on the market, the best choice for a touring binding was a 3-Pin, since it has no cable that encloses your heel while climbing and is super lightweight. Now with the new technology of the 7tm you have both the advantages of a 3-Pin and a cable binding combined, because for the ascent it allows you to minimize the pressure of the heel lever with a simple rim screw.

A very essential piece of equipment for ski touring is the so called climbing aid or bail. It allows you to lift your heel up to 4 cm for steep climbs and is simply switched up underneath the heel of your boot sole. An even more essential part of your touring equipment are the climbing skins, which are normally glued to the base of your skis and make it possible to climb with your boards. If it gets really steep and icy it becomes necessary to either take your skis off and walk or to fix crampons on your bindings.

Other essentials for ski touring and off-piste skiing are: an avalanche transceiver, a probe and a shovel - optional pieces of equipment for avalanche safety are: a so called ABS-backpack, which air balloons are inflating, if you get caught by an avalanche and release it. The inflated air balloons are supposed to keep you on the surface of an avalanche and should avoid getting buried. The Black Diamond Avalung vest enables you to breathe underneath the snow surface, if you have been buried and thus prolongs your life expectation in an avalanche, under optimal circumstances, for at least 1 hour.

 The best preparation for ski touring and safety awareness is a to attend a special avalanche training class. Offered by mountain clubs and climbing schools, you not only learn everything about avalanche rescue, but also where, how and why avalanches are released.

A deep snow run as a reward a for hard-earned ascent

As tempting as the adventure might be – responsible ski mountaineers are anything but high-spirited adrenaline junkies who venture a mountain without alpine experiences and insufficient equipment. Only if all safety aspects before and during a ski tour are taken into account, is it possible to enjoy the winter world of the mountains intensely, without risk and away from the crowd.

What I can do

- Short turn.
- Dynamic turn initiation (for example: jump turns).
- Skiing in different terrain and different snow conditions.
- Being in good physical shape.

What I have to know to plan a ski tour

- The personal prerequisite of the weakest member of the group is decisive.
- Every tour has to be planned and carried out according to the actual avalanche and snow situation.
- It is essential to evaluate the length and the vertical meters of the tour. You must not be totally exhausted if you reach the summit and want to start skiing – the safety risk and the danger of accidents for the whole group then gets too big.
- NEVER GO TO THE LIMIT!

Responsible Telemarkers are not thoughtless adventurers

What I need for a ski tour

- *Skins:* They should exactly fit on the skis, which is above all important for skis with a side-cut. There are skins on the market that are ready-made, however you should check the measurements exactly, because they have been cut by a computer only since the beginning of 2001. Today there are also skins on the market that you have to cut to size by yourself (e.g. Ascension by Black Diamond) – it only takes a little experience and manual skills.

  The best proved skins are those that you glue and strap on, the so called "glued strap-on skins". They are attached to skis with a tail clip and a rubber tip and get glued to the base of the ski. The skins are fitted such that there is a space of 1-1.5 mm on each side, which is the width of the edges.

  Check not only the skins, but also the tail clip and the rubber tip before you hit the trail – the latter must be wide enough to fit on the particular width of your ski tips.

- *Crampons:* They are used to avoid slipping in hard, icy and steep spots of the track, add to safety under such circumstances and are fixed either to the boots ore directly to the bindings. The only thing which still is awkward at the moment is the fact that there actually aren't crampons on the market which fit to the different types of bindings. So help yourself, get a pair of alpine ski touring crampons (e.g. for a Fritschi Diamir binding) and fix or glue 'em to your boots with straps or duct tape.

- *Adjustable Poles:* These poles can be altered in their length – for the ascent it should be at least waist-high, for skiing in deep snow a favorable length is "rib-high" or even longer, depending on the deepness of the snow. Another big advantage of some adjustable poles is the possibility to convert them into an avalanche probe (e.g. Black Diamond).

- *Avalanche Transceiver:* Never ski tour without one! It always should be worn as close as possible to your body (the best place is directly over your underwear) – carrying it in the pocket of your pants, underneath your jacket, or even worse, in your backpack, it could get torn from your body instantly in case of an avalanche release. Check your transceivers before every ski tour precisely! Therefore one of the group members sets his transceiver on "receive"

Jumps – Necessity or pure lust?

and all the others walk by him individually, at a distance of 5-8 meters with their transceivers set on "transmit". After this procedure, the one in the receive mode sets his transceiver to transmit and gets checked by another member of the group in the receive mode – if you receive a signal all the time, the transceivers are O.K.! And don't forget: Switch them back into the transmit mode after the check!

Before you are heading for the mountains, you should in any case practice with your transceivers at home – there is no time to read the manual in case of emergency.

- **Probe and shovel:** Without carrying a probe and a shovel a transceiver only has little value, since you can only roughly locate your buried partners, but can't dig them out!

- Other things you don't want to miss on a tour: First-Aid kit, maps, compass, altimeter, functional clothing, additional underwear, food and drinks, sunscreen, sunglasses and one of the above mentioned optional accessories like an ABS-backpack or a BD Avalung-vest.

Powder skiing − it should never end

How to behave on a ski tour

- Start slowly, find your rhythm and adapt the speed to your group, the weather and the terrain.
- Have a little break after the first 15-20 minutes, check your gear again and drink or eat a little something – after this you can keep on walking at a constant speed but always below your personal limit.
- Always keep your clothing adapted to the particular situation. You can start in the morning with an extra layer of fleece, or a windstopper jacket and take it off during the day, if it gets warmer. If the sun comes out, you don't want to forget your sunglasses and the sunscreen – something really important once you are above a height of 2500 meters in spring!
- During the tour you should always make sure that you eat and drink sufficiently – don't risk dehydration and concentrate on food like chocolate and energy bars, rather than on ham, cheese and other heavily digested meals.
- Take enough breaks to prevent exhaustion – don't forget that you still have to ski back down again and mostly in pretty challenging terrain!
- While walking, you should have your weight loaded mainly onto the ski that you are standing on – make sure you have weighted it equally, from the toes to the heel.
- The other leg only gets pushed forward and does not get lifted up – it saves a lot of power and does not make sense. Lifting your back leg and the connected ski is only indicated if you have to break a new trail.
- Make your steps as long as possible to economize your climbing – only exception: steep terrain.
- Maintain a flat ski while walking and thus get the whole length of the skin into the snow – try to keep your skis flat, even in steep terrain, your edges will not hold half as good as your skins!
- If you break a new trail, it is important to have the track on the same level, for both skis – they should lay parallel and leveled out in the track. Walking on different heights can be very tiring.
- Your poles are planted sideways for the stabilization of your steps, same as for a classic kick and glide technique in cross country skiing. If it gets steeper, it is of advantage to plant them a little further backward.

Safety first – a helmet always protects you, especially in the deep snow

- In a terrain steeper than 30° you have to do kick turns and switch backs, because otherwise your skins would not hold anymore. Make sure you do a perfect uphill kick turn before you go on a tour.
- According to the pretty large amount of gear that you need for ski touring, you mostly have to carry a pretty heavy backpack. Change your skiing especially in deep-, crust- or spring snow accordingly – since the heavy load of your pack would pull you too far backward, in case you try to ski "out of the backside", you have to try to shift your weight slightly forward. Thus the backpack has an even contact with your upper body and it is way easier to keep your balance even in unexpected situations.

Competitions are attracting a lot of sportsmen and -women

3.2.6 Competition and Telemark Racing

Competitions in alpine sports exert a fascination on athletes and spectators, ever since the time of Sondre NORHEIM. When he and his friends from the Telemark region of Norway were jumping over kickers, or were skiing down the Huseby Hill in Christiania (today's Oslo), both the skiers and the spectators enjoyed these performances and early ways of skiing competitions.

As in the case for alpine skiing, a regulated competition circuit also has developed over the years, on a national and international level, in the Telemark scene. The first world championships were held in the year of 1987 in Hemsedal, Norway and since then, they take place in different countries, regularly all over the world. But the races for the world's are not the only competitions for the Telemarkers – what comes first is a series of world cup races which are held in the Alps, Scandinavia and North America. Not to count the innumerable races on a national level, such as the Swiss, Austrian, German or the US championships.

Similar to alpine skiing, the competitions are held in different categories: Giant Slalom, Parallel Slalom, Classic and Sprint classic.

All four disciplines are supposed to prove the variety of the Telemark sport. This means that a Parallel or Giant Slalom always has a built-in jump, to demonstrate the affinity to ski jumping.

At a Classic or a Sprint classic race, the competitors also have to do a 360° (through a prepared circle), a jump and a short skating track, to get to the finish line. Another difference to alpine racing, are the judges at the gates, which are spread all over the racecourse. They check whether the racers pass the gates in a "clean" (meaning: Telemark) technique and position.

If namely the step change is not carried out continuously, or the distance of the step has not the minimum of a sole length, the racers collect penalty seconds. Same thing for the jump: If the landing is not carried out in a Telemark position, or the minimum width, which differs between 10 and 20 meters, they receive penalties, which are added up with the overall time at the end of the race.

Jumps underline the variety of Telemark races

The "royal discipline" for Telemarkers is the Classic race. In this competition the racer is demanded in three different categories: As a ski jumper, as a cross-country skier and as a giant slalom racer. In the gates, it counts to get through, as fast as possible and to collect as little penalties as possible. The jump, which is mostly located in the middle section of the race, is taken with maximum speed – first, to reach the minimum width, second to not lose too much forward momentum in the air.

Before the finish line, sometimes also as an interruption of the slalom, there is an obligatory skating section, which is between 800-1500 meters long. For being fast enough in this part of the race, the competitors are doing a Classic with super long skating poles, meaning that they are racing the gates without any pole plant at all.

A typical Classic race: a Giant slalom in the upper part, a 360° in the middle section with a jump right after, then another giant slalom with a 360° and finally a skating course to the finish line.

Besides the skating and the jumping, these Classic races are also garnished with one or two 360° turns through prepared circles and have an overall running time between 150 and 270 seconds.

Next to the classic, which was held for the first time in 1986 in Vradal, Norway, there is a so called Sprint Classic in the competition program since 1998. This race consists of the same elements the long Classic, with the difference that it is shorter and has two heats.

For the spectators these competitions are far more attractive, because they basically can overview the whole racecourse from one spot. A Sprint Classic normally has 20-25 gates, a jump, a skating section and a minimum of one

360° – the overall running time is about 60 seconds, the height difference 300 and 500 meters.

The giant slalom comes considerably closer to a classic alpine race, because the only Telemark specific component involved is the jump and the judges who are having an eye on the "clean" technique of the racers. Such a Telemark giant slalom has a height difference of 250-400 meters and also has two heats.

The Parallel slalom, at which two competitors race besides each other, is carried out in the so-called K.O.-system. The height difference has a maximum of 100 meters and the racers have a time limit of 25 seconds, after which they have to be through the 12-18 gates.

Both speed and technique are important for successful Telemark racing

Fun and action are the main motivation for most Telemarkers in a competition

Until the 1997-98 season there was a strict regulation about the skis a Telemarker could use in a race.

The rule was that the skis maximum width had to be 73 mm and the minimum 63 mm. This rule got canceled in the meantime and now, also Telemarkers have the freedom of choice to race on race carvers in any length and width. The only rule that still exists is that in an official FIS-race, they have to wear a helmet and use a releasable safety binding.

If you want to try racing by yourself one day, you don't have to compete against the top 30 right away – almost every race has a so called fun-class (for hobby racers) and a master-class (for racers over 30 years of age), in which pure fun and action are playing the main role.

What I can do
- Skiing on the edge.
- Equal weight on both skis.
- Quick step change.
- Skiing with a bent hip.
- nitiating a turn not with a prerotation, but with a tilt.
- Short and long radius turns.

What I want to learn
- Skiing without a pole plant.
- Skiing in a constantly low position.
- Front knee almost straight.
- Very quick turn initiation.

What I have to do
- No vertical movement, thus a constant pressure on the edges, a safe and compact position and less air resistance.

Compact position of a Telemark racer

- No pole plant: Use your poles only to stabilize yourself between the gates.
- Step change in a low overall position, meaning that your legs swing through underneath your body.

- Keep your ski on the edges almost all the time.
- Quick step change.
- Equal weighting of both skis. Both skis are under permanent pressure and therefore have a better bite on a hard and icy slope.
- Upper body is slightly prerotated, but turn initiated by tilting into the center of the turn.
- Strongly bent hip, resulting in a strong pressure on the edges.
- Turn is skied from "behind" – front leg almost straight, thus the inside ski receives more pressure.

Both skis are weighted

How I can learn it

- Ski carving turns with a strong steering component on a regular slope.
- Ski on your edges without poles or without a pole plant.
- Ski without a vertical movement (keep a low stance).
- Ski with an extremely bent hip.
- Ski with a straight front leg.
- Ski along a given track through mini-gates.
- Slalom gate training.

With a bent hip, you maximize the pressure on your edges

4 TELEGUIDE

Actually Telemarkers only need a little snow and a little hill for their free heel experience, 'cuz basically you can Telemark in every ski area around the world. Nevertheless, there are a few spots which have developed into places where you meet more freeheelin' soul brothers and sisters than anywhere else – that's the reason to introduce some of our favorite resorts in North America and in the Alps.

North American Ski Resorts

Lake Tahoe, California: How many Californians does it take to screw in a light bulb? Takes four – one to screw in the bulb and three to join the experience. Another thing the Golden State has to offer next to an ancient hippie and esoteric culture is awesome skiing in some of the most attractive ski resorts in the States. Our #1 choice is Squaw Valley. This huge ski area which covers six different mountains and it's bowls, cliffs and steep runs, has earned the reputation of being the cradle of free skiing – check out the KT. 22 ! If you are going for some tree and powder skiing you don't want to miss Alpine Meadows and Heavenly including the crowds of freeheelin' locals. No complaining 'bout bearded wool sweaters in leather boots – they rip. Big time.

www.californiasnow.com

Breckenridge, Colorado: This is the place to be if "ya can't git enuff" and still want to ski soft and dry snow until the end of June. Being the highest ski resort in North America, it has T-bars that lift you up to the incredible height of 12,141 feet and offers premium off-piste skiing in one of the seven double Black Diamond runs of this place. Mr. Unparalleled himself, Paul Parker, lives here. Need to say more? Pero no.

www.breckenridge.com

Crested Butte, Colorado: If Squaw is the cradle of free skiing, Crested Butte is the cradle of the Telemark skiing of our days. This place is away from the hype and trendy mainstream of so many other ski resorts in Colorado and is packed with freaks from all over. It still has a lot of these days when sex was safe and freeheel skiing was dangerous – a little cowboy town which once was populated by a huge hippie community and now offers a great deal of on- and off-piste, as well as backcountry skiing, for affordable prices. Basically granola is only served for breakfast.

www.crestedbutte.com

Jackson Hole, Wyoming: Ten out of ten male inhabitants chew tobacco and ride pick up trucks, five out of ten ride horses, whereas the other five are free skiers and their local ski club is the "Jackson Hole Air Force".

Go on top of the Rendezvous Mountain, read the warning signs and then take off for some premium steep and deep hard core runs – Corbet's Couloir is only one of them. If you are looking for loads of ungroomed powder in a less steep terrain, you only have to head west to Grand Targhee and you are in the place to be.

www.jacksonholechamber.com

Germany

Garmisch-Partenkirchen: Since two thirds of the Telemarkers in Germany come from the south and since the Zugspitz is the only glacier ski area in Germany, it is crystal clear that the German Telemark scene mainly gathers in Garmisch-Partenkirchen. It's less the groomed slopes around the Zugspitz, which are the most attractive, but mainly all the neat little couloirs, deep snow and freeride runs, along with the nightlife, which turn this place into a little Chamonix of the eastern Alps.

www.garmisch-partenkirchen.com or www.zugspitze.de

Dammkar: The Karwendelbahn cable car takes you from Mittenwald to a height of 2,244 m into the first official free ride resort of Germany. From here, you have an ungroomed slope of 7 km length, down through the wild and breathtaking Dammkar, with a descent of 1,200 vertical meters and pure skiing fun. Who wants to be informed in time about the next powder alarm can register under the address listed below.

www.dammkar.de

Austria

St. Anton: This place offers one of the biggest freeride resorts in the whole eastern Alps – sweet snow, sweet chicas, sweet bars and horrible prices. Loads of Scandinavians and freeriders from all over the world give this place a special something and raise the average skill level by a hundred and ten percent.

www.arlberg.or.at
or
www.stantonamarlberg.com

Stubai glacier: The best glacier in the eastern Alps, which offers skiing in all kinds of terrain, for at least 2 months longer than any other glacier area in this part of Europe. The highest lift station is at 3,056 m and once you have found a bunch of Telemarking locals (this place is packed with freeheelers) to show you around, you'll want to stay the rest of the season. Friendly lift attendants, good food, pretty stable weather conditions and at least two Telemark events a season. Check out the Dorf Pub in Neustift!

Kleinwalsertal: A nice little spot in the remote part of the Allgäu-Alps, with a pretty neat tele-scene and one big event in every season: The official German Telemark Championships, with a three day side event and the opportunity to test the latest material and your ability to process between 2-3 liters of German beer, in 24 hours. Check out the *Walmendingerhorn* area!

www.kleinwalsertal.at or www.kanzelwand.at

Switzerland

Engelberg: This place is undoubtedly the #1 Telemark resort in the Swiss Alps – it is not only home to the oldest Telemark club in Switzerland, but also has to offer innumerable world class off-piste and freeride runs around the *Titlis* (3,239 m). You find Telemarkers all over the place and it's your own fault if you still ski by yourself after a whole day in this crowd.

www.engelberg.ch

Verbier: Okay, the lift lines are a little longer from time to time here in Verbier, but it's worth waiting to get to the top. Because if you are finally standing on top of the *Mont Fort* and see the legendary "Stauseeabfahrt" , than you forget all about the dead boring line. But also the *Mont Gele*, or the *Col de Mines* and the *Vallon d'Arbi* (you can reach both via the Lac de Vaux lifts), are awesome off-piste runs. These innumerable free ride runs and the outstanding nightlife in Verbier are definitely a reason for Telemarkers from all over the world to spend their winter here in the Quatres Vallees.

www.verbier.ch

Zermatt: Who skis off-piste a lot and who likes high alpine ski touring in the spring has, without question, a full score in Zermatt – the place to be. This huge ski area has to offer an incredible number of awesome free ride runs. Check out the *"Haus Telemark"* next to the Kleinmatterhornbahn for a stylish accommodation.

www.zermatt.ch

France

La Grave: One cable car, one t-bar lift and 2,000 m of pure fun: La Grave actually is a tiny little mountain village, but who has ever taken the gondola up to 3,200 meters and then the t-bar up to 3,500 meters, has a rough idea of what this place is all about. Once you are on top, you have 2,000 vertical meters of premium off-piste terrain ahead of you. Even if the last snow fall was a couple of days ago, you still find runs with waist deep powder and places you have never been before. No worries if you are way too tired to go for some nightlife after a day of skiing – there isn't any.

www.la-grave.com

Chamonix: The opposite of La Grave according to size and infrastructure – here you meet Telemarkers from all over the world in the breathtaking scenery of Mont Blanc, Grand Jorasses and Mer de Glace. Go find a local or a guide to show you around, because this place offers extreme Telemarking at its best.

www.chamonix.com

Val d'Isere: Val d'Isere and Lac de Tignes did join together to an awesome and giant ski area, whereas for Telemarking, Val d'Isere is our spot of choice: An incredible number of off-piste runs, which are all within reach of a lift or cable car and with a snow quality, that has no equivalent in the Alps. If the conditions are right, you have the option to go tree skiing in the so called Le Fornet Trees; also try *Col du Montet, Pointe Pers, Pente de Lores* and *the Couloirs 1, 2* and *3* in Tignes.

Italy

Livigno: That Livigno is the Mecca of the Telemark world, is a fact for everyone who once was lucky enough to join the legendary La Skieda. There is no other place in the world where so many Telemarkers gather in one place at the same time – the whole thing is a party that lasts for 8 days and probably the best thing that ever happened after Woodstock. (Trust me, I'm local.)

www.skieda.com

Norway

Hemsedal: It is something like an obligation for every Telemarker to ski in Norway once in his lifetime – our favorite place: Hemsedal. Maybe not the #1 resort in Norway, but it definitely has the best parties and the most laid back and cool Telemarkers all over.

www.hemsedal.com

5 OUTLOOK

ou can take one thing for granted – Telemarking is far more than another fun sport. This skiing technique rather looks back at about 150 years of tradition, and we are proud of it. Ignorant critics keep asking us why nothing modern, or new would occur to us and why we always have to go back to the past. However, we, the freeheelers, like this look back over the shoulder – we are walking forward and at the same time don't forget where we are coming from.

And this is the reason why Telemarking became a life philosophy for so many skiers. One day they have tried their first turn in the step position mainly out of curiosity – and were infected.

Then they got addicted an intoxicated, because Telemarking simply is the pure bliss and for a lot of us the ultimate kick.

Telemarking will never evolve into a fashion sport like snowboarding – but who wants it to? Do we want to get our sport as commercialized as the whole boardin' thang? No, by no means never, ever.

We rather draw our lines away from the crowd and enjoy the snow and the winter world of the mountains in small groups or with a bunch of friends – and this is without any question something you cannot experience as intensively as on tele-boards. We are the ones who can do everything with simply one pair of skis and boots – carve the groomed, climb the powder mountains, skate over distances like a cross-country skier and even jump and land everything in our way.

Since the revival of Telemark skiing until the 1990s, it was restricted to only a few good skiers to fly down slopes and powder runs in the old Norwegian style. With the up until then common material (leather boots, 3-Pin bindings and super narrow skis), it simply took a good and experienced alpine skier to really ski with this kinda stuff. When the first plastic boots, along with the wider skis and the release bindings came onto the market, this niche kind of sport did not turn into a real boom, but into a constantly growing trend, which attracts more and more people. Now we are facing no more limits that are set by the material.

Moreover, Telemarking came back to life within the last few years – no matter whether it is a racer with a skintight suit and a helmet, a traditionalist with a loden coat, hat and leather boots, or a free rider in a GoreTex-outfit and duct taped plastic boots – they are simply all part of the Telemark community.

Without any question the Telemarkers have pushed a new door open in winter sports ever since the revival over 25 years ago. We will see how many skiers will make it through that door – the only thing that we can do is to keep on freeheelin' and bring Telemark to the people.

"Free your heel, your mind will follow."

6 LITERATURE AND MEDIA TIPS

BÄHNI M./BATTANTA, P./ZURBUCHEN, M.: Swiss Telemark. The Spirit of Skiing. Video VHS, Magglingen 1997.

KLEPPEN, H.: Telemarkskiing – Norway's Gift to the World. Oslo 1986.

O'BANNON, A./CLELLAND, M.: Allen & Mike's Really Cool Telemark Tips. Canada 1998.

PARKER, P.: Free-heel-skiing. 2nd edition, Seattle 1995.

RYERSON, N.: P.D.Q. – Telemark Technique. Aspen 1997.

Internet Addresses:

www.telemarktips.com
www.couloirmag.com
www.powder-works.com
www.powdermag.com
www.upproductions.com
www.telemarkbuch.de
www.telemarkfriends.com

Our thanks go to the following companies for their support:

Powder Works
Arnold Sport
Da' Bergbaron
Haus Telemark (Zermatt)

7 THE AUTHORS AND THE TEAM

Patrick Droste

The Authors

Patrick Droste, born in 1964 and qualified sports instructor, works as a sports editor for a newspaper in Hamm, Germany and is a qualified Telemark instructor of the DSV (German Ski Association).

Ralf Strotmann

Ralf Strotmann, born in 1963, works as a sports and mathematics teacher at a high school in Olpe, Germany.

Both authors have competed as members of the master class in national and international competitions and are leaders of the resort "Nordic skiing" at the SPORTS association for ski and sports instructors. Together they already have published two books about Telemark skiing.

Uta Rademacher   *Peter Musch*

Photographer and Translator:

Peter Musch (Munich)

Drivers:

Ueli Bäerfuss
Wolfgang Glasmeier
Mathias Hediger
Masa Inagaki

Frank Obermaier
Yvonne Peters
Jan Schapmann
Andy Schimeck
Peter Stannecker

Photographers:

Uta Rademacher (Berlin)
Andreas Rother (Werne-Stockum)
(page 134)

8 PHOTO & ILLUSTRATION CREDITS

Coverphotos:	Uta Rademacher und Peter Musch
Photos:	Uta Rademacher und Peter Musch
Photo on page 134:	Andreas Rother
Illustrations:	Yvonne Peters
Coverdesign:	Birgit Engelen, Stolberg

Make a Perfect Start